DATE DUE

MY 11'98			

DEMCO 38-296

Religion and Suicide
in the
African-American Community

Religion and Suicide in the African-American Community

KEVIN E. EARLY

Forewords by
RONALD L. AKERS
and
ROBERT DAVIS

Contributions in Afro-American and African Studies, Number 158

GREENWOOD PRESS
Westport, Connecticut • London

ıtion Data

....nerican community / Kevin E.
Early ; forewords by Ronald L. Akers and Robert Davis.
       p.   cm.—(Contributions in Afro-American and African
studies, ISSN 0069-9624 ; no. 158)
    Includes bibliographical references and index.
    ISBN 0-313-28470-9 (alk. paper)
    1. Afro-Americans—Suicidal behavior. 2. Afro-Americans—
Religion. 3. Suicide—Religious aspects—Christianity. I. Title.
II. Series.
HV6545.5.E37   1992
362.2′8′08996073—dc20   92–19425

British Library Cataloguing in Publication Data is available.

Library of Congress Catalog Card Number: 92–19425
ISBN: 0–313–28470–9
ISSN: 0069–9624

First published in 1992

Greenwood Press, 88 Post Road West, Westport, CT 06881
An imprint of Greenwood Publishing Group, Inc.

Printed in the United States of America

∞™

The paper used in this book complies with the
Permanent Paper Standard issued by the National
Information Standards Organization (Z39.48–1984).

10 9 8 7 6 5 4 3 2 1

Copyright Acknowledgments

The author and publisher gratefully acknowledge permission to use copyrighted material.

Permission to reprint "For Black Poets Who Think of Suicide" by Etheridge Knight
granted by Broadside Press.

Every reasonable effort has been made to trace the owners of copyright materials in this
book, but in some instances this has proven impossible. The author and publisher will
be glad to receive information leading to more complete acknowledgments in subsequent
printings of the book and in the meantime extend their apologies for any omissions.

We Wear the Mask

We wear the mask that grins and lies,
It hides our cheeks and shades our eyes,—
This debt we pay to human guile;
With torn and bleeding hearts we smile,
And mouth with myriad subtleties.

Why should the world be over-wise,
In counting all our tears and sighs?
Nay, let them only see us, while
We wear the mask.

We smile, but, O great Christ, our cries
To thee from tortured souls arise.
We sing, but oh the clay is vile
Beneath our feet, and long the mile;
But let the world dream otherwise,
We wear the mask.

—Paul Laurence Dunbar

Contents

Tables

Foreword

Ronald L. Akers
University of Florida

One of the founders of sociology, Emile Durkheim, showed us long ago that the ultimate private act, suicide, does not result solely from private, pathological factors. He focused on social forces in suicide as part of his efforts to define social facts, *sui generis*, as the core of the discipline of sociology. Suicide has remained one of the defining issues in sociology. In addition, it continues to be a major social problem for which society seeks answers and solutions. Media attention to suicide contagion among teenagers, the right-to-die movement, and notorious cases of doctor-assisted suicide have kept the problem of suicide in the public eye. We want to know not only about social forces that promote suicide, but about social structures and processes that may counter or prevent suicide.

Kevin E. Early's study has implications for understanding suicide both as a central sociological issue and as an important social problem. He turns our attention to answering the question of why black suicide rates have been and remain so low compared to white suicide rates. As he reminds us, the probability of white Americans taking their own lives, in spite of some recent increases in suicides among younger black males, is about twice that of African Americans. Why should this be? Many of the indicators of anomie, deprivation, desperation, and hopelessness, which one line of theory proposes are factors in suicide, are high in the African-American community. This community does suffer disproportionately as victims and perpetrators of crime and drug abuse. Yet it does not suffer disproportionately from suicide. What characteristics of the black community relatively insulate it from suicide, and why do these characteristics seem not to insulate it as much from other social problems?

These are the powerful and important questions to which Early seeks relevant answers. He makes no claims to definitive conclusions. His is an exploratory study in one community, and there are other acknowledged limitations of the research. Nevertheless, he offers intriguing findings in support of the hypothesis that the religiously based normative climate in the black community acts as a buffer against suicide. He also uncovers in his interviews with black pastors and a survey of their congregations subtle variations in this climate regarding crime and drug abuse.

Whether readers agree or disagree with the theory, methodology, or conclusions of this study, it will command their attention. It is an important contribution to our knowledge of suicide. Sociologists and interested nonsociologists alike will find this book to be a valuable resource.

Foreword

Robert Davis
North Carolina A&T State University

Between the time of the publication of the pioneering work of Charles Prudhomme, "The Problem of Suicide in the American Negro" (1938)[1] to Kevin E. Early's *Religion and Suicide in the African-American Community*, there have been few informative and sociologically useful interpretations of suicide within the black community. Historically, suicide among blacks has never been a real and serious concern for the handful of sociologists and psychiatrists specializing in suicide research. Only a few behavior scientists' careers have touched the lives of suicidal black people. The explanations offered by these researchers are at best patronizing, depicting the weakness of the black family, a history of authority problems with the police, retroflective anger, and other distorted psychosocial patterns as being central factors in black suicide. This paucity of empirical studies designed to evaluate theories about causes of black suicide has been accompanied by a general lack of suicide prevention programs and strategies targeted specifically at the black community.

Why have research scholars and behavioral scientists ignored self-destructive behavior in the black community? Many argue that the reason is because of the lower rates of completed suicide among blacks. However, I suspect that the answer lies in the political nature of research funding and the fact that suicide among blacks does not have priority in terms of research and program planning among majority scholars.

There are few useful explanations for why the black suicide rate has been relatively low and stable over time. Kevin E. Early's book offers an answer to the above question that is firmly grounded in the sociological literature on suicide. *Religion and Suicide in the African-American Community* integrates Durkheimian functionalism with Blumer's symbolic interactionism and focuses on the shared social meaning of suicide in the black community and the influence of church-based news as a buffer against suicide.

The view that social bonds, social integration, and primary group relations are important factors that buffer against suicide was represented in original form in Emile Durkheim's *Suicide* ([1897] 1951). Durkheim focused on the individual's attachment to social groups and their goals and the extent to which the individual was regulated by the collective conscience. Durkheim's law states that suicide varies inversely with the degree of integration of the individual into the group.[2] He saw vulnerability to suicide in people who were not integrated into any religious communal or family group. Modern proponents of this theory maintain that a disruption of social relations is the primary causal factor in suicide and that supportive significant others function as a buffer to immediate suicide threats.

For the most part, Durkheim's sociological approach to suicide and applications of his theory neglected the issue of black suicide. However, the theoretical framework utilized in Kevin Early's work allows a limited empirical test of Durkheim's buffering hypothesis. *Religion and Suicide in the African-American Community* focuses on the part played by the church in constructing and reinforcing a particular social meaning of suicide (attitudes, norms, values, and beliefs) that may act as a counter to or guard against suicide.

In terms of methodology employed, the book is primarily an exploratory ethnography that draws on the tools of participant observation, face-to-face interviews, and traditional survey research. Early's curiosity about the social functions of the church led him to explore via these methodological tools how the black church functions to provide refuge from despair, account for the uncertainties of life, inspire hope, and renew confidence to face the challenges of everyday life.

Early's discussion of the effects of such "protective factors" as strong religious beliefs and extended family life is in the tradition of previous studies of the black community (see Billingsley, 1968; Hill, 1972; and McAdoo, 1981).[3] He examines the views of pastors and members of their congregation in an attempt to document the existence of a consistent, normative climate, into which individuals are socialized through the church and family, that is staunchly anti-suicide or that provides a social meaning of suicide as repugnant and perhaps even unimaginable.

Early concludes that the church's influence creates buffers against suicide among blacks and that church leaders and members alike "condemn suicide as an unpardonable sin, as a 'white thing' alien to the Black experience."

The manner in which Early captures the flavor and tenor of the church-based attitudes and norms regarding suicide is another major strength of this volume. Suicide is defined as unpardonable, unforgivable, and even unthinkable for blacks. The church recognizes no justification for suicide. To the extent, then, that this shared social meaning of suicide radiates out into the black community, Early suggests that it plays a role in keeping the black suicide rate low, thus allowing the conclusion that empirical support exists for the working hypothesis with which *Religion and Suicide in the African-American Community* began. This qualitative ethnographic study of the socially integrative, suicide-buffering normative climate operating in the black church and radiating out to the larger black community is an important contribution to the literature on suicide.

NOTES

1. C. Prudhomme, "The Problem of Suicide in the American Negro," *Psychoanalytic Review* 25 (1938): 187–204, 372–91.

2. Emile Durkheim, *Suicide*, ed. George Simpson (1897; reprint, Glencoe, IL: Free Press, 1951).

3. A. Billingsley, *Black Families in White America* (Englewood Cliffs, NJ: Prentice-Hall, 1968); R. Hill, *The Strengths of Black Families* (New York: Emerson Hall, 1972); H. McAdoo, *Black Families* (Newbury Park, CA: Sage Publications, 1981).

Preface

The rate of suicide among African Americans is about half that of white Americans. Why is the rate so low? One hypothesis is that the black church's influence is an essential factor in that it ameliorates or buffers social forces that otherwise would lead to suicide. This book, the first ethnographic study that looks at the buffering effect of the black church against suicide, investigates the empirical support for this hypothesis. (The terms black, black American, and African American are used interchangeably.)

The specific theoretical framework for this book follows one line of interpretation from French sociologist Emile Durkheim's theory of suicide. In this interpretation, the place of African Americans is anomic and disorganized, and suicide should be more prevalent than it is.

Data were collected through face-to-face interviews with pastors of black churches and through a survey questionnaire completed by black church congregations. Interviews with pastors included general questions about their views of suicide and elicited their responses to four vignettes portraying suicide situations, crime, and drug abuse. Additionally, a questionnaire survey was administered to congregation members to elicit their attitudes, opinions, beliefs, and feelings concerning suicide. Findings from the data indicate a consensus among pastors and congregations. Pastors and a majority of their congregation members condemn suicide as an unforgivable sin, and as a "white thing" that is alien to them—a denial of what it means to be black.

The theoretical framework, a review of the literature on African-American suicide, and the working hypotheses are outlined in chapter 1. A discussion of the results of this investigation is presented in chapters 2, 3, and 4. Conclusions, limitations, implications of the study, and recommendations for future research are discussed in chapter 5. Research questions, sampling and data-collection procedures, and analytic techniques are described in the appendices.

The findings are consistent with the hypothesis that the church provides a normative climate that helps to keep the black suicide rate low. Limitations of the study and suggestions for future research are presented. The theory-guided research reported here goes beyond what is currently available in the literature. This research should provide a basis for further testing of the tentative conclusions, and should suggest a basis for future research for such testing.

Acknowledgments

I am indebted to many individuals, first of all Ronald L. Akers, colleague, friend, and mentor, who has broadened and deepened my understanding of sociology. I have valued his scholarly and practical insights. I have also benefitted immensely from the encouragement and feedback of my colleague Robert Davis. Bob gave me direction that laid the foundation of the book.

Special thanks go to my colleagues at Oakland University in Rochester, MI—John K. Urice, dean of the College of Arts and Sciences; Isaac Eliezer, associate dean of the College of Arts and Sciences; David J. Downing, associate dean of the College of Arts and Sciences; Thomas F. Kirchner, administrator for College Services; and Jacqueline R. Scherer, chair of the Department of Anthropology and Sociology—for making available resources that allowed me to complete manuscript revisions.

I thank Sherry S. DuPree, reference librarian at Santa Fe Community College, Gainesville, Florida, and Richard Newman, manager of publications at the New York Public Library, for encouraging me to write this book, and for their comments and suggestions about the manuscript.

I am grateful to Ken Kochanek, National Center for Health Statistics (NCHS), who provided me with NCHS documents, for which I am most appreciative.

Several people were instrumental in helping to improve the quality of the final manuscript. Deborah Szobel Logan edited seemingly endless drafts of the manuscript, always with patience, competence, and a good sense of humor. I want to thank my colleagues Peter Bertocci, William Bezdek, Judith Brown, James Dow, Harry Gold, Susan Hayworth-Hoeppner, Albert J. Meehan, Gary Shepherd, Richard Stamps, and Donald Warren of Oakland University, and Henry C. Lacey, Dillard University, for their encouragement, support, and helpful suggestions for improving the manuscript. Other people helped me at various points in the project by providing able technical assistance, including Peggy M. Bensett, Seema H. Bijlani, Miranda K. Brockhaus, Judith Brownlee, Michigan Department of Civil Rights Library; John J. Coughlin, Kevin P. Lambrix, James D. Llewellyn, Robert J. Manning, Nadia Martin, University of Michigan Taubman Medical Library; Padmakumar, Darlene Roach, Winfred I. Robinson, Michael J. Shields, Kenneth E. Waddell, Judy Watkins, Detroit Public Library; and Tzuu-tao Weng.

Gratitude is expressed to James T. Sabin, executive vice president of Greenwood Publishing Group, Inc., and the staff for the interest and attention given to this book.

This book would not have been possible without the patience and support of my wife, Bonnie, who has been a great source of support, encouragement, and love.

Finally, I am grateful to all of the individuals whose experiences are recorded in these pages.

Religion and Suicide
in the
African-American Community

Chapter 1

Theoretical Framework

The forces contributing to African-American suicide have received relatively little attention from research scholars, most likely because the rate of suicide in this group is comparatively low. While this stance is understandable if attention goes to where problems are most acute, it is not sociologically defensible. Varying rates of suicide across racial groups are, in fact, a compelling reason to focus attention on both high- and low-rate groups. Why is there relatively little black suicide? One answer offered by scholars is that religion and family in the African-American community ameliorate or buffer social forces that otherwise would promote suicide.

This book will investigate the extent to which the above answer is a good one. Specific focus will be on the part played by the church in constructing and reinforcing a particular social meaning of suicide (attitudes, norms, values, and beliefs) that may act as a counter to or buffer against the higher rate of suicide that would be expected to result from the social forces involved in forms of deviance such as crime and drug use.

This study is not able to define how important religion has been in keeping the black suicide rate low, and no systematic comparisons with the white community or white religious groups are made. The study does provide a basis for at least tentative conclusions about a religiously based normative climate or set of social meanings and expectations in the black community that define suicide as especially unacceptable or unthinkable for blacks.

The social meaning of suicide includes the norms, values, attitudes, and beliefs regarding suicide, and the response to suicide and suicide attempts in the religious community. The argument is made that these views are not confined to the religious community, but are shared by the larger black community. This view differs from Douglas' (1967) investigation of the social meaning of suicide, which concentrated on the communicative patterns leading to specific meanings of suicide for individuals prone to suicidal actions. Ultimately, the social meaning of suicide in the black community is communicated to black individuals. But the focus here is on the content of the shared social meaning in the black community rather than on the individual's process of acquiring those meanings.

The emphasis on church-based views of suicide stems from the church's crucial role in holding together the social fabric of the black community. The church is a strategic place in which to explore the social meaning of suicide in the black community because of the historical centrality of the institution of religion and its relation to the family and social life in that community. This centrality does not mean that the influence is one-way. The social meaning of suicide in the church in part reflects some secular beliefs and the place of blacks in American society.

The literature describes the influence of the church as pervasive in the black community. Therefore, the moral and social views promulgated by church leaders and adhered to by active church participants should be influential in the views of the black community, including those on suicide. I do not attempt to demonstrate this influence in the community studied, but the assumption of the centrality of the black church is common in the literature and is stated unequivocally by the church leaders in this study. Urban sociology, the study of the African-American family, and the study of the African-American community all point to the church as a key element of the African-American community. Modern sociological theory clearly defines religion as a crucial part of the social fabric of the African-American community. This book is primarily an exploratory ethnography that draws upon (1) the researcher's experience as a participant in the religious life of the African-American community; (2) semistructured interviews with pastors of established black churches; and (3) questionnaire responses from church members.

THEORIES OF SUICIDE

Recall that the theoretical framework utilized here follows a line of interpretation from Emile Durkheim. Durkheim's sociological approach to suicide always has aroused the considerable interest of research sociologists. For the most part, however, the applications of his theory and the research designed to test it have neglected the issue of African-American suicide. But when the issue is engaged, Durkheim's influence is apparent.

By the time Durkheim attempted to explain and classify suicide in the late nineteenth century, empirical correlations had been firmly established attributing suicide rates to a wide range of social factors (e.g., race, heredity, imitation) and, to a lesser extent, individual factors such as mental disorder (Giddens, 1965, pp. 3–15; Douglas, 1968; Turner and Beeghley, 1981). It is important to view Durkheim's classic 1897 study, *Suicide*, in the context of the developed tradition of European thought concerning suicide (Durkheim [1897] 1951).

"The originality and vitality of Durkheim's study did not lie in the empirical correlations contained in his work" (Giddens, 1965, pp. 3–15). Such empirical correlations already had been documented by writers such as Legoyt, Morselli, Ottingen, and Wagner (Giddens, 1965, pp. 3–15). Durkheim's study was an outgrowth of these earlier works. Durkheim used ideas such as "egoism" (detachment from structural relations in groups) and "lack of moral restraint" as variables in determining suicide rates (Giddens, 1965, pp. 3–15; Turner and Beeghley, 1981, pp. 354–55).

Durkheim's major contribution was to reformulate ideas already advanced by theologians, philosophers, and psychologists into a sociological theory of suicide that "became the standard reference for all subsequent sociological interest in suicide" (Akers, 1985, p. 287). In *Suicide*, Durkheim's primary objectives were to explain such an individual behavior as suicide as a sociological phenomenon and to "make a persuasive case for the importance of the discipline of sociology" (Ritzer, 1988, p. 16; Wekstein, 1979, p. 27).

From Durkheim's perspective, suicide is a phenomenon whose causes are contingent primarily upon the nature of an individual's integration into the group's social fabric and on the ability of the group to regulate its members. Durkheim assumed that humans were selfish and in need of regulation. He posited that the group was the source of the regulation of the selfish drives and needs of the individual. Durkheim attended to both innate biological drives that needed to be regulated (e.g., sex drive) and to socially created wants that needed to be controlled (e.g., material success). In fact, Durkheim suggested that the socially created needs were more difficult to control because they were potentially limitless. One can continually desire more money if making money is the end rather than the means to satisfy other needs.

Durkheim focused on the individual's attachment to social groups and their goals, and the extent to which the individual was regulated by the collective conscience. Attachment "involved the maintenance of interpersonal ties and the perception that one is a part of a larger collectivity," and regulation "limited individual aspirations and needs, keeping them in check" (Turner and Beeghley, 1981, p. 353).

What was unique to Durkheim's sociological interpretation was that he saw rates of suicide as a social fact. Durkheim stated:

> If . . . the suicides committed in a given society, during a given period of time are taken as a whole, it appears that this total is not simply a sum of independent units, a collective total, but is itself a new fact *sui generis*, with its own unity, individuality and consequently its own nature—a nature, furthermore, dominantly social. (Durkheim, 1951, p. 46)

Conforming to Durkheim's definition, suicide has a reality apart from the individual (Durkheim, 1951, p. 46). It is manifested as a collective tendency or, in Durkheim's terms, "suicidogenic" impulses (Durkheim, 1951, p. 210). According to Durkheim, the "suicidogenic" impulses differ from one society or collectivity to another. Such impulses are the determining causes of suicide (Durkheim, 1951, p. 210). Each society is "predisposed to contribute a definite quota of voluntary deaths. This predisposition may therefore be the subject of a special study belonging to sociology" (Durkheim, 1951, p. 51).

Durkheim developed a method of classifying the causes of suicide based on the nature of the individual's relations to the normative structuring of the collectivity in which he is located (Parsons, 1968, pp. 311–319; Turner and Beeghley, 1981, p. 353). He proposed four categories of suicide: (1) egoistic, due to a weakening and loss of close social ties to groups and collectivities; (2) anomic (normlessness), the result of deregulation of the individual's desires and passions; (3) altruistic, the result of the individual's integration into the group being so excessive that the individual commits suicide for the good of the group; and (4) fatalistic, the result of "excessive regulation, that of a person with futures pitilessly blocked and passions violently choked by oppressive discipline" (Durkheim, 1951, p. 276; Wekstein, 1979, p. 27; Turner and Beeghley, 1981, pp. 353–55; Little, 1983, p. 142). These categories are based on the degree and nature of the integration of the individual into the social collectivity. "The degree of a person's integration into social life and the amount of regulation over his behavior were keys to understanding suicide rates" (Little, 1983, p. 142).

Egoistic suicide is the name given by Durkheim to suicide resulting from poor or absent social (family, religious, state) ties of the individual into groups or collectivities (Durkheim, 1951, pp. 152–217; Wekstein, 1979). The individual "is not well integrated into the society and life has become meaningless" (Little, 1983, p. 142). Thus, the suicide rate is reduced where individuals are closely integrated with their societies.

Durkheim also used religion to illustrate egoism. He observed that suicide rates vary by religious denomination. Historically Catholic countries have a lower suicide rate than historically Protestant countries. The Catholic religion, according to Durkheim, has a stronger common conscience as well as a traditionally established, closely woven set of beliefs and rituals into which the life of the individual is well integrated (Durkheim, 1951, pp. 152–70). Conversely, the Protestant church is less ritualistic and more individualistic. "The Protestant is far more the author of his faith" (Durkheim, 1951, p. 158). As such, a high degree of individual responsibility emerges. The Catholic church emphasizes integrating its members into church relations and rituals that may act as a buffer against suicide.

Durkheim also observed that suicide rates in poor countries are lower than those in affluent ones; that people not involved in a marital relationship tend to have a higher suicide rate than those who are married; that the larger the family, the more "integrated" a person is; that suicide rates are adversely affected by national crises; and so on (Durkheim, 1951, pp. 171–217; Little, 1983, p. 141). Suicide, according to Durkheim, varies inversely with the degree of social integration of the collectivity to which the individual belongs (Durkheim, 1951, p. 209; Aron, 1967; Turner and Beeghley, 1981, pp. 352–56; Akers, 1985). "Durkheim therefore reasoned that if suicide rates showed consistent patterns among social categories, there must be social characteristics to explain the consistencies" (Little, 1983, p. 141).

Altruistic suicide, due to excessive identification and integration, results from an excessive sense of duty to the society (Durkheim, 1951, pp. 217–41). In other words, social integration is too strong and thwarts individual identification. "It is the group that is paramount, with individuals subordinating their interest to those of the group" (Turner and Beeghley, 1981, p. 354).

Social conditions favoring anomic suicide arise "as the result of deregulation of individuals' desires and passions" (Turner and Beeghley, 1981, p. 355). In a state of moral deregulation, the "society's influence is lacking in the basically individual passions, thus leaving them without a check-rein" (Durkheim, 1951, p. 258). Anomic suicide is an outgrowth of moral deregulation. Fatalistic suicide arises from the individual's excessive regulation (Durkheim, 1951, p. 276). It is, according to Durkheim, "the suicide of very young husbands, of the married woman who is childless" (Durkheim, 1951, p. 276). It is also the suicide of slaves. However, fatalistic suicide "has so little contemporary importance and examples are so hard to find aside from the cases just mentioned," that Durkheim does not deal with this type of suicide (Durkheim, 1951, p. 276).

Other writers have attempted to categorize suicide. For example, Halbwachs (1971) rejected Durkheim's typology of egoistic-altruistic suicides and anomic-fatalistic suicides (Giddens, 1965, p. 7). According to Halbwachs, the "social isolation" of the suicidal individual is the real cause of suicide (Giddens, 1965, p. 7). Hence, one can expect suicide rates to be high in social environments (e.g., metropolitan centers) "promoting the detachment of individuals from stable relationships with others" (Giddens, 1965, p. 7).

Johnson (1965) agrees with Halbwachs that the "two variables of regulation and integration which Durkheim saw as independent social causes of suicide turn out to be just two labels for the same thing" (Akers, 1985, p. 292). He rejects the theory's major problem, which, according to Johnson, arises out of Durkheim's proposition that the suicide rate depends on two variable social conditions, that is, social regulation and social integration (Johnson, 1965, p. 876). Although the two determine the incidence of suicide in any group, "Durkheim seldom locates a group in both dimensions at once" (Johnson, 1965, p. 881).

Johnson regards egoism (integration) and anomie (regulation) as one dimension instead of two. Egoism and anomie are two different names for the same concept (Johnson, 1965, p. 882). "A well-integrated group is also well regulated, and even using Durkheim's own concepts, anomie and egoism cannot be clearly distinguished" (Akers, 1985, p. 292; Johnson, 1965, pp. 882–84). Hence, "Durkheim is left with 'only one cause' of suicide: lack of social integration" (Akers, 1985, p. 292). "The more integrated (regulated) a society, group, or social condition is, the lower its suicide rate" (Johnson, 1965, p. 886). Conversely, the less integrated/regulated a society, group, or social condition, the higher its suicide rate.

Such interpretations of Durkheim, which focus on social integration and anomic suicide, have guided subsequent studies. But not all subsequent suicide studies have been guided by this "one-cause" argument. Rather, they have maintained the types and different causes as defined by Durkheim. In these studies emphasis is placed on anomie/egoism and altruism/fatalism as primary determinants of suicide. Both lines of reasoning have influenced research on black suicide, as we shall see in the next chapter.

All modern American sociological theories and studies of suicide have been heavily influenced by Durkheim, but neither Durkheim nor later theorists pay sufficient attention to black suicide. Are black suicides simply expressions of fatalism, as Durkheim's brief reference to suicide and slavery would suggest? Do integration and regulation, in Durkheim's terms, keep egoistic and anomic suicide rates low in the African-American community? Is the same explanation for suicide in modern society in general applicable to suicide among African Americans?

At this stage, there are no generally accepted answers, because of a relative dearth of studies on African-American suicide. This lack does not mean that the issue has been ignored, but that Durkheim's relative inattention to African-American suicide (or race variations in suicide) has been carried into modern literature on suicide. Before turning to a review of recent theory and research on African-American suicide, I will examine briefly the extent to which the suicide rate is lower for blacks than for whites.

DIFFERENCES IN BLACK AND WHITE
SUICIDE RATES

Suicide rates for African Americans have been consistently lower than white suicide rates for both sexes and all age categories, as shown in Table 1.1. Overall, the white suicide rate (13.4 per 100,000 in 1988) is about twice the black rate (6.7 per 100,000 in 1988), as shown in Table 1.2.

Table 1.1 shows that the suicide rates of whites are higher than those of blacks in every age group. For white males, suicide increases linearly with age. White female suicide rates are related curvilinearly to age. They increase until age seventy-four; thereafter they decrease.

Conversely, black male rates decrease with age, but increase slightly after age sixty-four. However, "there is some evidence that the rate actually increases among blacks up to the age of 34 and [then] drops off sharply" (Blackwell, 1985, p. 334; Davis, 1980a, pp. 223–29). Black female suicide rates decrease with age. Clearly, the highest suicide rate within the black population occurs among young adult males (Blackwell, 1985, p. 334; Davis, 1980b, pp. 223–29).

The suicide rate in 1986 among black males ages twenty-five to thirty-four was 21.3 per 100,000, compared to 26.4 per 100,000 for white males in the same age group. At no other age are the black and white suicide rates so close. The U.S. Census Bureau reports that suicide is the third leading cause of death among African-American males ages twenty-five to thirty-four, after homicides and accidents. The above is also true for white male suicide rates in the same age group, but the suicide rate for white males continues to increase with age, while the black rate peaks in this age category.

Increases in African-American male suicide during the 1980s have been matched by increases in the white male rates. The white male rate of suicide averaged 1.8 times higher and the white female rate averaged 2.5 times higher than those of African-American males and females respectively (Department of Health and Human Services, 1991; National Center for Health Statistics, 1992). Therefore, while the black suicide rate has increased during the past two decades, it still does not approximate the white rate (see Table 1.2).

Table 1.1
Suicide Rates Per 100,000 According to Sex, Race, and Age, 1950–1989

	1950	1960	1970	1980	1983	1984	1985	1986	1988	1989
WHITE MALE										
15–24 yrs.	6.6	8.6	13.9	21.4	20.6	22.0	22.7	23.6	23.4	23.2
25–34 yrs.	13.8	14.9	19.9	25.6	26.2	25.8	25.4	26.4	25.7	24.9
35–44 yrs.	22.4	21.9	23.3	23.5	23.2	23.7	23.5	23.9	24.1	23.8
45–54 yrs.	34.1	33.7	29.5	24.2	25.5	25.3	25.1	26.3	23.2	24.2
55–64 yrs.	45.9	40.2	35.0	25.8	27.4	28.8	28.6	28.7	27.0	26.6
65–74 yrs.	53.2	42.0	38.7	32.5	33.2	35.6	35.3	37.6	35.4	35.1
75–84 yrs.	61.9	55.7	45.5	45.5	52.5	52.0	57.1	58.9	61.5	55.3
85–	61.9	61.3	50.3	52.8	56.8	55.8	60.3	66.3	65.8	71.9
BLACK MALE										
15–24 yrs.	4.9	4.1	10.5	12.3	11.5	11.2	13.3	11.5	14.5	16.7
25–34 yrs.	9.3	12.4	19.2	21.8	19.1	20.7	19.6	21.3	22.1	22.0
35–44 yrs.	10.4	12.8	12.6	15.6	14.0	16.5	14.9	17.5	16.4	18.1
45–54 yrs.	10.4	10.8	13.8	12.0	12.1	11.6	13.5	12.8	11.7	10.9
55–64 yrs.	16.5	16.2	10.6	11.7	11.6	13.4	11.5	9.9	10.6	10.4
65–74 yrs.	10.0	11.3	8.7	11.1	13.6	13.8	15.8	16.1	12.9	15.4
75–84 yrs.	6.2	6.6	8.9	10.5	15.8	15.1	15.6	16.0	17.6	14.7
85–	6.2	6.9	10.3	18.9	12.7	11.1	7.7	17.9	10.0	––

WHITE FEMALE

Age										
15–24 yrs.	2.7	2.3	4.2	4.6	4.6	4.7	4.7	4.7	4.6	4.4
25–34 yrs.	5.2	5.8	9.0	7.5	7.2	6.6	6.4	6.2	6.1	5.9
35–44 yrs.	8.2	8.1	13.0	9.1	8.2	8.4	7.7	8.3	7.4	7.1
45–54 yrs.	10.5	10.9	13.5	10.2	9.9	10.0	9.0	9.6	8.6	8.0
55–64 yrs.	10.7	10.9	12.3	9.1	9.1	9.1	8.4	9.0	7.9	7.9
65–74 yrs.	10.6	8.8	9.6	7.0	7.9	7.8	7.3	7.7	7.3	6.4
75–84 yrs.	8.4	9.2	7.2	5.7	6.6	6.8	7.0	8.0	7.4	6.3
85–	8.9	6.1	6.1	5.8	5.3	5.1	4.7	5.0	5.3	6.2

BLACK FEMALE

Age										
15–24 yrs.	1.8	1.3	3.8	2.3	2.7	2.4	2.0	2.3	2.6	2.8
25–34 yrs.	2.6	3.0	5.7	4.1	2.9	3.5	3.0	3.8	3.8	3.7
35–44 yrs.	2.0	3.0	3.7	4.6	3.5	3.2	3.6	2.8	3.5	3.9
45–54 yrs.	3.5	3.1	3.7	2.8	3.0	3.5	3.2	3.2	3.8	3.0
55–64 yrs.	1.1	3.0	2.0	2.3	1.7	3.1	2.2	4.2	2.5	2.5
65–74 yrs.	1.9	2.3	2.9	1.7	1.3	2.5	2.0	2.8	2.0	—
75–84 yrs.	2.4	1.3	1.7	1.4	1.3	0.5	4.5	2.6	1.3	—
85–	—	—	3.2	—	2.3	0.8	1.4	—	0.0	—

Source: National Center for Health Statistics, *Vital Statistics of the United States*, Vol. II, *Mortality, Part A, 1950–89* (Hyattsville, MD: Public Health Service, 1992).

Table 1.2
Suicide Rates Per 100,000 According to Race and Sex, 1970–1989

Race and Sex	1970	1980	1985	1986	1987	1988	1989
TOTAL	11.8	11.9	12.3	12.8	12.7	12.4	12.2
Male	17.3	18.6	19.9	20.6	20.5	20.1	19.1
Female	6.8	5.5	5.1	5.4	5.2	5.0	4.8
WHITE	12.4	12.7	13.4	13.9	13.7	13.4	13.1
Male	18.0	19.9	21.5	22.3	22.1	21.7	21.4
Female	7.1	5.9	5.6	5.9	5.7	5.5	5.2
BLACK	6.1	6.0	6.2	6.5	6.6	6.7	7.0
Male	8.0	10.3	10.8	11.1	11.6	11.5	12.2
Female	2.6	2.2	2.1	2.3	2.1	2.4	2.4

Sources: Department of Health and Human Services, *Statistical Series, Annual data, 1990*. Series E-21 (Washington, DC: U.S. Government Printing Office, 1991); National Center for Health Statistics, *Vital Statistics of the United States*, Vol. II, *Mortality, Part A* (Hyattsville, MD: Public Health Service, 1992).

TWO PERSPECTIVES ON SUICIDE

As mentioned previously, Durkheimian theory can be applied in at least two ways to black suicide. The first perspective includes modern anomie theorists who see deviance of all kinds, including suicide, as flowing from disjunctures in the opportunity structure in, or from the cultural goals and social structure of, society. This perspective is sometimes referred to as strain theory by its proponents (Merton, 1938; Cloward and Ohlin, 1961).

The second approach is associated with the Chicago School, a group of University of Chicago sociologists during the 1920s and 1930s whose ideas remain influential to this day (Gold, 1982, pp. 23–26). Social disorganization theorists of this school attributed deviance of all kinds to rapid social changes that lead to weakened social norms or social control. Lewis Wirth, for example, hypothesized that as the size, density, and heterogeneity of urban populations increased, the character of social organization and social relationships would also change. The division of labor would become more elaborate and complex, the bonds between residents would grow weaker and more impersonal, superficial, transitory and anonymous. Their lives would be lived at a faster pace, and their contacts with other people would become more superficial.

Thus, Wirth and other members of the Chicago School saw personal disorganization, mental breakdown, suicide, delinquency, crime, and social disorder as products of the rootlessness of growing urbanization (Gold, 1982, p. 127). According to Little (1983, pp. 15–16), economic deprivation is anomic or disorganizing. Therefore, higher rates of crime, mental illness, suicide, drug abuse, and other deviance should be highest in lower-class and disadvantaged groups and communities.

Neither Wirth nor Little adopts Durkheim's strong social control assumption, in which the needs and wants of individuals must be regulated by the social group. Durkheim expects uncontrolled human selfishness to lead to crime and deviance; the selfishness does not have to be specially motivated. In contrast, both the modern functionalist theories and the social disorganization approaches see social structural arrangements as generating or motivating deviance that otherwise would not occur (see Liska, 1981).

Modern anomie theory proposes that disintegration or disorganization produces high rates of all forms of deviance, not just suicide. The social disorganization approach of the Chicago School expects high rates of all types of deviance, including mental illness and depression.

Cavan (1928) attributed suicide to the amount of social or personal disorganization experienced by the individual. "Suicide was explained by disorganization (i.e., powerlessness and hopelessness) in the community or in the life of the individual" (Akers, 1985, p. 289). Hence, black suicide rates should be high because anomie and social disorganization are believed to be pervasive in the black community. Merton's (1938) version of anomie theory proposed a means-ends theory to explain high rates of deviance.

In this "strain" theory, lower-class and minority groups are denied equal opportunity to legitimate means in pursuing the "American Dream" (Akers, 1985, p. 23; Little, 1983, pp. 16–17). Unable to achieve cultural goals of success, individuals turn to illegitimate, criminal, and delinquent means.

According to Merton, then, communities, societies, or social groups are apt to be anomic where the discrepancies between cultural ends and means are exacerbated. For African Americans, a forced division of labor has reduced blacks to a lower-class status, thereby creating conditions for a breakdown of norms, or anomie. As such, Merton's proposition should predict among blacks high rates of suicide, as well as other forms of deviance (e.g., delinquency, crime, homicide, incarceration, and drug addiction).

Cohen's (1955) version of anomie theory would argue that deviance is the result of status frustration, that is, of poor individuals' inability to meet the demands of middle-class standards. Status frustration produces a subculture in which middle-class values are inverted (a reaction formation) so that subcultural values are opposed to the very middle-class values that inspired them. Although Cohen's theory was applied specifically to delinquency subculture, it viewed the lower-class neighborhoods as anomic.

Similarly, Cloward and Ohlin (1961) ascribe higher rates of deviance in the lower-class subculture to an "opportunity structure." In other words, deviance is said to result from blocked opportunity and deprivation. Blocked legitimate opportunity structures produce strain toward deviance. Thus, the same conditions of anomie are felt to prevail and to produce high rates of all forms of deviance. However, like Durkheim (1951, p. 162) and Henry and Short, Cloward and Ohlin distinguish between self-blame, which results in deviance, and blame of others (or alienation, according to Cloward and Ohlin), in which anger and frustration are focused outward. From this perspective, deviance in the black community may be high since blacks experience overwhelming deprivation of economic, social, and political means to cultural goals, but suicide may be low because blame is directed outward.

The literature on black suicide reflects this disorganization and anomie theme. For instance, Clark (1965), Schultz (1969), Glasgow (1981), and Wilson and Aponte (1985) propose that the rapid deterioration of black institutions brought on by racial integration, assimilation, and urbanization has increased social disorganization and fostered increased suicidal behavior among African Americans. Holinger and Offer (1982) agree, arguing that the competition for opportunities that exists between African Americans and their white counterparts results in alienation of blacks and eventual suicide. The figures reported in Tables 1.1 and 1.2 support the argument that black suicide rates have increased, but show that white rates also have increased.

The theories within this anomie/disorganization tradition (with the exception of Cloward and Ohlin) would expect high rates of suicide and deviance among African Americans. While other deviance may be high in the black community, suicide is not. If anomie theory is correct, then, something is counteracting the disorganization and strain factors in the black community. The hypothesis as adumbrated in the first chapter is that the church provides an integrative normative climate that differentially affects suicide versus other forms of deviance. If a buffering effect exists, then the black church is key in providing it.

A second perspective on suicide more closely follows the original Durkheim theory of integration and regulation. Henry and Short (1965) propose that "external restraints" contribute to high rates of outward aggression. "They accept the hypothesis that aggression is the inevitable result of frustration and postulate that both homicide and suicide are aggressive products of frustration" (Little, 1983, p. 146; see also Akers, 1985, pp. 289–90).

Henry and Short begin with the question: Why is there a tendency for people in some social categories (e.g., blacks) to have high homicide rates and low suicide rates while others (e.g., whites) have low homicide rates and high suicide rates? When external restraint is strong, frustration produces aggression that is directed outward in violence toward others rather than at oneself. Lower status (for lower-class people, minorities, and women) means greater external restraint and thus lower suicide rates. Similarly, Maris (1969) explains suicide in terms of the lack of social integration and subordinate status, which he terms "external constraint." The greater the external constraint, the lower the probability of suicide.

Because of the division of labor (in fact, a forced division of labor results from *de jure* and *de facto* discrimination), black Americans have been relegated to a low status. Hence, aggression for blacks "in a racially stratified society is more likely to be directed outwardly than inwardly" (Little, 1983, p. 147). Nowhere is this outward frustration/aggression more evident than in the black community, where the "evidence includes the high incidence of drug abuse, crime, Black-on-Black murder, imprisonment, and mental illness" (Moss, 1991, p. 292).

From this perspective, at least some structural aspects of economically and socially deprived communities are seen as predictive of low rates of suicide. Rather than proposing that economic disadvantage was anomic, Durkheim viewed poverty itself as regulative as long as the poverty was viewed as just (Durkheim, 1951, pp. 248–54, pp. 382–84). Poverty "protects against suicide because it is a restraint in itself" (Durkheim, 1951, p. 254).

If black poverty in the United States is largely a result of discrimination, then one must attend to the structure of the forced division of labor that created and sustains the impoverished conditions. When groups are subjected to a forced division of labor, group solidarity (and regulation) does not match the organic solidarity that develops from a spontaneous (i.e., unforced) division of labor premised on merit (Durkheim, 1933). The collective conscience, then, can be expected to survive among oppressed groups. The collective conscience refers to a shared consciousness that has a life of its own apart from the individuals who produce it.

In the black community, one might look for indicators of mechanical solidarity that survive as part of the collective conscience. This results from the collective experience of a forced division of labor. Thus, as members of the black community experience conditions of a forced division of labor, a collective conscience emerges reflecting that experience.

In "mechanical societies the collective conscience is religious in content and that integrates the individual into the collective" (Turner and Beeghley, 1981, pp. 357–58). Turner and Beeghley suggest that religion is the place to find indicators of the collective conscience. Therefore, it is important to examine black religion to see what it says about suicide. The low black suicide rate may reflect a strong group consensus that condemns suicide. Durkheim's empirical indicator of the collective conscience in *The Division of Labor* is law. But to the extent that the law is "white," it cannot be used to study black solidarity in conditions of a forced division of labor.

Durkheim clearly saw the function of religion in a traditional, less differentiated society—it insulated against egoism, which was the primary source of suicide in the white European society of his day (Durkheim, 1951, p. 356). Moreover, Durkheim's theory of egoism was particularistic. It explained only suicide, not other forms of deviance and crime (Durkheim, 1951, p. 356). In fact, Durkheim argued that where suicide is high homicide may be low because the two arise from antagonistic causes (Durkheim, 1951, p. 356). Durkheim also maintained that the prophylactic effect of religion against egoism was due not to the content of beliefs about the value of life or the prospects of condemnation, but to the social integration that religion fosters (Durkheim, 1951, p. 170).

The forced division of labor provides another avenue for extending Durkheim's theories to black suicide. The overcontrol and regulation of the present-day forced division of labor has elements of what Durkheim briefly referred to as "fatalism." However, Durkheim (1933) suggested that when overcontrol results from a forced division of labor, the oppressed can be expected to strike back at their oppressors when subjugation is eased. Under such circumstances, suicide might be low (depending on the collective conscience) and other deviance high. Durkheim saw no tendency toward all forms of deviance where there is a forced division of labor and fatalism (Durkheim, 1951, pp. 338–60).

Durkheim devoted only a footnote to fatalistic suicide, but others whose theory is close to Durkheim's tend to view black suicide as fatalistic (Breed, 1970). It is not clear whether this interpretation would expect fatalism to be prevalent enough to predict high rates of black suicide, but if so, the church could counter fatalism by offering a philosophy of hope.

An investigation of the role of religion in black suicide is in order with regard to either the first perspective, based on anomie and disorganization, or the second, which maintains the Durkheimian typology of suicides. However, the literature that cites the church as an important factor in low black suicide rates tends to follow the anomie/disorganization perspective. In this literature, the place of blacks in American society is viewed as anomic. Deprivation and blocked opportunities place on the black community strain that should produce high rates of all forms of deviance, but the church and other institutions provide internal integration and act as buffers against suicide.

RELIGION AS A SUICIDE BUFFER IN THE AFRICAN-AMERICAN COMMUNITY

Since Charles Prudhomme's pioneering work, "The Problem of Suicide in the American Negro" (1938), few empirical studies have been conducted on black suicide. Modern literature begins with the idea that blacks who commit suicide are overwhelmed by feelings of powerlessness and oppressive discipline (Davis, 1980b, pp. 228–29; Little, 1983, p. 142; Gibbs, 1988, p. 272; Moss, 1991, p. 292). "The experiences of depowerment, powerlessness, alienation and anomie have fallen to the individual level to understand, interpret and resist" (Moss, 1991, p. 292).

Anomie, in the modern sense of disjuncture between goals and means, or social disorganization, is viewed as high among African Americans. Every indicator of social disorganization (e.g., dysfunctional families, powerlessness, high illegitimacy rate, alienation, unemployment, blocked opportunity) and the supposed consequences of drug abuse, crime, and delinquency characterize the black community. From this perspective, it is reasonable to ask: Why do African Americans have a low rate of suicide in the face of a high level of social disorganization?

The answer given in the literature is that alienation and anomie do not result in high suicide rates because features of the black community, such as strong religious beliefs and extended family, buffer or "protect" against suicide. Billingsley (1968), Stack (1974), Allen (1978), Martin and Martin (1978), and McAdoo (1981) look at factors such as family, church, social organizations, schools, and social support systems that they believe insulate African Americans from suicide. Rutter (1985) uses the term "protective factors" to describe the relationship between the aforementioned institutions and African-American suicide.

The above studies (as well as Davis, 1980a) propose that "the likelihood of suicide is increased without important support systems." Bohannan (1960) proposes that black suicide rates are lower than white rates because of stronger social ties. Woodford (1965) suggested that urbanization, integration, and racism have served to immunize African Americans against suicide by producing adaptability. Davis (1980a) proposes that suicide among African Americans is "likely to occur under conditions of weakened relations, i.e., loosening or weakening of communal and family ties." However, Davis also offers the buffering hypothesis:

> For blacks, the stresses and anxieties that might lead to suicide have often been offset by strong family and communal ties. Effectively denied all other mechanisms to compensate for rejection and abuse, blacks have in the past used their families, communities, and institutions (i.e., churches, social clubs, fraternal organizations, etc.) to develop positive and functional forms of response to recur-

rent stressful social situations. The black community, in effect, has functioned as a protective society, providing participation and purpose, a sense of belonging, and the possibility of cooperative and self-help approaches to problems. (Davis, 1980b, p. 228)

The hypothesis in the literature is that social forces that buffer against suicide are found in the values and norms of the African-American church and family. Religion and the church have provided unification and leadership, and the African-American family has been amazingly resilient, under extraordinarily stressful and debilitating conditions (Wilson, 1988). Strong family ties and traditions have persevered through the separation, disruption, and disorganization of slavery, economic and social changes, mass migration, mother-only families, and economic deprivation.

Unfortunately, little empirical support exists for how the above factors actually account for the lower black suicide rate. Davis (1980b) refers specifically to the paucity of empirical studies designed to evaluate theories about causes of African-American suicide or about why the rate is lower than that of whites. This study is meant to fill some of that empirical gap.

The working hypothesis here is that the church is an important source of social integration and of norms that act as buffers against suicide. This is not to say that such resources are insufficient in the white community—there is no intent at this time to make any systematic comparisons between African Americans and their white counterparts.

The purpose of this study is to examine the extent to which the norms and social processes that are consistent with the buffering hypothesis exist in the African-American community. To propose that the church in the black community acts as a buffer makes intuitive and sociological sense. Therefore, I treat as a working hypothesis the exploration of a relationship between the black church and the low rate of black suicide. The research does not include the precise testing of this hypothesis for its definitive acceptance or rejection. But this study does serve as a starting point and basis for future research. Is there an identifiable set of religiously based beliefs about suicide that would buffer against suicide among African Americans? If so, what are those beliefs? Why do they prevent suicide but not other forms of deviance?

Church leaders within the African-American community, by and large, are local residents. They are religious, moral, and social leaders. Although many of the African-American church leaders are not college-educated or seminary-trained, and are not affiliated with national religious groups, they still occupy positions of respect in their communities. This localism adds to the community-oriented nature of African-American churches, as well as to their involvement in political and social movements.

By fulfilling multiple functions, the church has been an integrating and unifying institution around which even the nonreligious rally. Most churches within the African-American community come from within the local community: African Americans essentially form their own churches. The churches are for the most part indigenous neighborhood churches that support each other and the family and help to unify social bonds within the community.

The state of knowledge in this area of research is still very much in the exploratory stage. This research focuses on at least one aspect of the black community that may counter suicide: a consistent, normative climate, into which individuals are socialized through the church and family, that is staunchly anti-suicide or that provides a social meaning of suicide as repugnant and perhaps even unimaginable.

Chapter 2

The Role of the Church

For Black Poets Who Think of Suicide

Black Poets should live—not leap
From steel bridges, like the white boys do.
Black Poets should *live*—not lay
Their necks on railroad tracks, (like the white boys do.
Black Poets should seek, but not search
Too much in sweet dark caves
Or hunt for snipes down psychic trails—
(Like the white boys do;

For Black Poets belong to Black People.
Are the flutes of Black Lovers—Are
The organs of Black Sorrows—Are
The trumpets of Black Warriors.
Let all Black Poets die as trumpets,
And be buried in the dust of marching feet.

—Etheridge Knight

GENERAL ATTITUDES, BELIEFS, AND VALUES REGARDING SUICIDE

Recall that the intent here is to investigate the social meaning of suicide in the black community. In particular, the study focuses on the possible role of church norms and social relations in promoting, constructing, and reinforcing in the black community a particular social meaning that counters or buffers against the higher rate of suicide that would be expected to result from the same social factors that foster other forms of deviance such as crime and drug abuse. The literature suggests that the church and its interaction with the family have been major influences in keeping the rate of suicide among African Americans relatively low, but no direct empirical investigation has been made.

This study is not able to define the importance of religion in containing the black suicide rate, and no systematic comparison with the white community or religious groups is made. The study does provide a basis for at least tentative conclusions about the empirical reality of a religiously based normative climate or set of social meanings and expectations in the black community that defines suicide as beyond the pale, as especially unacceptable or unthinkable for blacks.

The social meaning of suicide includes the norms, values, attitudes, and beliefs that prevail in the black community, as revealed in the religious community's teachings about and responses to suicide and suicide attempts. The church is a strategic place in which to explore the social meaning of suicide in the black community because of its historical centrality and its relation to the family and social life in that community.

If the influence of the church is pervasive, then the moral and social views promulgated by church leaders and adhered to by active church participants should be influential in the views of the black community, including views on suicide. The pastors interviewed for this study were asked not only to relate their own opinions, but also to address directly the issue of suicide in the black community as compared to other deviant acts such as drug abuse and crime. The interviews were loosely structured to concentrate on the following issues: religious and normative views toward suicide; the role of the black family in religion, and of religion in the black family and wider community; the extent to which suicide-relevant norms and attitudes are transmitted in church; and the causes and prevention of suicide and suicide attempts in the black community. The findings and conclusions from the pastors' responses to questions in these four areas will be presented in this chapter. The central place of the church in the black community and its unity with the family will be addressed first. Findings in the other three areas will be presented next, pointing out that the views transmitted by the pastors reveal a deep sense of the incompatibility of suicide with the black experience.

As we shall see later, there is a consensus among these informants. While it was not possible to assess how thoroughly this consensus is shared throughout the community, a sample of church participants (presented in chapter 4) was surveyed to judge the extent to which they share the pastors' views.

THE CENTRALITY OF THE CHURCH IN THE AFRICAN-AMERICAN COMMUNITY

The church has played a major role in the African-American experience. The church has "traditionally been the central axis around which the rest of the community revolved" (Gibbs, 1988, p. 352). For African Americans, the church "has served as a refuge for blacks from racial discrimination and social oppression," and has been the conferrer of status, the center of organization, and the center of protest (Gibbs, 1988, p. 352; Staples, 1976). The civil rights movement of the 1950s and 1960s was largely church-led, and many of its participants are today's black leaders: the Reverend Ralph Abernathy, congressional delegate Walter Fontroy, Dr. Joseph Lowery, the Reverend Jesse Jackson, and former United Nations ambassador Andrew Young.

C. Eric Lincoln (1974) perceptively and vividly describes the unique place of the church in the black community:

The Church is the spiritual face of the Black community, and whether one is a "church member" or not is beside the point in any assessment of the importance and meaning of the Black Church.

Because of the peculiar nature of the Black experience and the centrality of institutionalized religion in the development of that experience, the time was when the personal dignity of the Black individual was communicated almost entirely through his church affiliation. The Black Church, then, is in some sense a "universal church," claiming and representing all Blacks out of a long tradition that looks back to the time when there was only the Black Church to bear witness to "who" or "what" a man was as he stood at the bar of his community. The Church still accepts a broad-gauge responsibility for the Black community inside and outside its formal communion. "The Church" is still in an important sense "the people," and the Church leaders are still the people's representatives. (Lincoln, 1974, p. 116)

Feagin (1989) adds:

After the Civil War, churches played an important role in black communities. Churches were mutual-aid societies, ministering to those facing sickness and death, and they played a role in the pooling of economic resources. Education often came as religious education. New schools were established after the war, many under religious auspices, and some trained ministers as black leaders. Black churches continued as community and schooling centers, since few such centers were provided by local or state governments. (Feagin, 1989, p. 246)

As C. Eric Lincoln and others have long recognized, church leaders in the African-American community have been more than just religious figures. By and large, they have served as moral, social, and political leaders as well. Therefore, the values, norms, attitudes, and beliefs of African Americans—not just those actively involved in church—have their origin in the church.

If the church is to provide social integration and moral values that will pervade the African-American community, then its role must go beyond the religiously active. The present study, based in Gainesville, Florida, cannot demonstrate that the majority of black citizens in and around Gainesville recognize such a role for the church. However, the church leaders interviewed in this study (identified by the numbers that indicate the interview date and number) echo and support Lincoln's and others' view of the church as an institution with unifying and leadership roles in the black community. They point to the black church as an institution that has provided social and cultural integration for black Americans, and has interacted with the black family to provide resilience under stressful conditions.

[Interview 08269010] The church has played a major role because it has been the Bible of the black community from slavery time to now. The thing that has held us together has been the church and prayer. The church has been the social hall. It's been the place of contact. It's been the place to where the meeting of the minds take place. I see the suicide rate very low in our community compared to others because of the role that the church has played. It has helped blacks understand. It has built self-esteem. It has helped educate them as to what would happen and the result of suicide. The belief of heaven and hell really existed. The facts of eternity. The facts of lost people and saved people. I think that the part that the church has played in training, developing, and creating the minds of our young people has been a vital part of really holding the community together.

[Interview 08169008] I think religion is the greatest aspect of the black community. It's the greatest thing going. When you come to religion you are equal. The church is the black person's life. That's where most of everything is taken care of anyway. Our politics are taken care of at church. That's when we decide who to vote for. In education, the pastor tells you to get back in school. In economics, bills are even discussed with the pastor. Religion is the fiber of our community. If we lose that, we're gone. It is what's holding us together.

Another pastor agrees, and emphasizes that the church fulfills social as well as religious functions, bringing together in the church activities and community participation that spread out among several organizations operating in the white community:

[Interview 07149001] Well, first of all, the black church is our only communication. The black people have nothing else. They don't have any women's clubs. They don't have any decent recreational facilities. Uh . . . they don't have any Jaycees or business clubs. Whereas, the white community has all kinds of outlets where they can express themselves and let off their steam. The black people only have the church.

Another pastor explains the same view and emphasizes the importance of the church as a refuge, as a problem solver and integrator in the face of difficulty:

[Interview 07149002] We don't own anything. We don't produce anything. They have it all. The only thing we have is the church. It has been our only refuge in times of storm . . . in times of struggle . . . it's all we have. The Word through the church . . . uh . . . I believe has kept us from destroying ourselves. The church tells us to live life and weather out the storm. Brighter days are ahead and coming. We are the heartbeat of each family. The black church historically has been the life blood of the black people.

Historically, the church has acted as the political, social, religious, and moral voice of the black community. This multiple function of the church, together with its interplay with the family, supports the idea that "The Church" is in an important sense "the people" (Lincoln, 1974, p. 116). The nature of this relationship helps to unify social bonds within the black community.

The power of the black church in the black community is embedded in the "nature of the black experience and the centrality of institutionalized religion in the development of that experience" (Lincoln, 1974, p. 116). African Americans possess a social and religious way of life that provides individuals with group acceptance and support and a method for discharging stress. The church affects not only the life of its active members but the life of the larger black community.

Among African Americans, religion by itself is cited as the factor that most influences their day-to-day life and their sociopolitical and cultural behavior. The most observable aspect of the

African-American's life, religion is much more integral to the black community than to the white community—it clearly permeates black society. Staples (1976) describes religion as representing African Americans' social reality:

> Religious worship brings about the sharing of beliefs and practices by a group with a common history and a shared destiny. The religious experiences in Black churches serve the purpose of giving strength, identity and a reason for being to its members. It provides a structured world view and a system of defense and attack in a basically hostile environment. (Staples, 1976, pp. 165–66)

Theologian and professor Gayraud S. Wilmore adds:

> Black religion has always concerned itself with the fascination of an incorrigibly religious people with the mystery of God, but it has been equally concerned with the yearning of a despised and subjugated people for freedom—freedom from the religious, economic, social, and political domination that whites have exercised over blacks since the beginning of the African slave trade. (Wilmore, 1983, pp. ix–x)

As Staples and Wilmore recognize, it is through religious participation that morals, ethics, self-definition, and cultural traditions are expressed. Attitudes, values, and patterns of social organization also are learned.

In a real sense, then, African Americans are a religious people. This notion is so ingrained into the fabric of African Americans that it has succeeded in developing a collective consciousness, with regard to many aspects of life, among African Americans. Religious participation and devotion are believed to enhance the quality of life both in this world and in the world to come after death. This assumption in the black community allows individuals to "achieve relief from their oppressed condition" (Staples, 1976, p. 166). Given the centrality of the church and the significance of religion in the black community, it is reasonable to expect that the views of suicide held by black religious leaders have an effect on the views and behavior of that community.

THE BLACK CHURCH AND THE BLACK FAMILY

For both white and African Americans, the church and family are intertwined. Among African Americans, though, the family and church are especially integrated as a unit responsible for addressing social, economic, and political needs and problems. Perhaps not uniquely, but in a special way, the family and church are the primary, twin pillars of African-American society. This structure is a historical and traditional extension of African culture, as well as of the African slave experience in the United States. The extended family has been a significant element in the survival and advancement of African Americans. Religious services were one of the few reasons for which slaves were allowed to congregate. Hence, the influence of the extended family has provided conditions under which primary socialization and the influence of religion have occurred. This feature not only has made the black family the primary socialization and learning unit, but has allowed it to become resilient to the socioeconomic conditions of poverty, unemployment, and scarce economic resources (Stack, 1974, p. 124).

No data or analyses specifically or separately involving the black family were a part of this study. However, given the close ties between the religious and family institutions, informants were asked about the relationship between the church and the black family. The black family is seen by blacks as the primary socializer, while white families tend to have other avenues for socialization. Religious participation through the church is essential in promoting individual and communal growth and development; the black family is seen as an effective socializer and haven of support that diffuses or prevents the stress that may result in suicide.

[Interview 07179003] The Afro-American family was structured so that we were taught by watching parents in terms of how they handled their stresses and pressures. We were taught that there is a better way out than doing suicide; finding someone to help. The white family structure has never been and never will be as strong as the Afro-American structure. There was things within the Afro-American family structure that we were taught in terms of respect. In terms of knowing to seek those who were older than you. In terms of just being who you were, but staying in your place until such time as you were ready to handle such pressures and stresses. On the other hand, whites have allowed their children not to be children and brought up that way, but to somewhat fit right into the mainstream of being adults the minute they thought they were old enough to understand all of the ramifications of life which no child or teenager can understand. Those were things that were kept from us. We were asked to stay in our places and that has helped us not to reach out and grab for the world so fast and become bogged down with these pressures and stresses as whites have. That's why I feel that suicide rates among Afro-Americans is just not as great.

The church is portrayed as an extension of the family. Indeed, the prevailing attitude of the pastors in this study is that the church and the family are one unit. "The church is our mother, shield and our only hope" (Interview 07149002).

The role of the church is to promote the social, educational, occupational, and political aspirations of the black community. The family's role is so intertwined with the church's that it is hard to determine where one ends and the other begins. In the words of one pastor:

[Interview 09039011] The black family and religion are one and the same. The role of religion in the black community is to give meaning, purpose, and direction to our lives. This is why you find blacks gathered at the black church where the gospel is preached, prayer is made, and scripture is taught. You will find answers there.

The pastors interviewed in this study go to great lengths to explain the church's role within the black family. According to the pastors, the church acts as the intercessor between family and community. "The role of the black church is to keep the family together. The church is also there to educate, inform, and help as much as possible. That has always been the role of the black church throughout the ages" (Interview 07149002).

Because the family and church are seen as one entity, the church sets the standards for how the family is to function within the community. In the words of one pastor, the black church "acts to keep the black family in a group. All of the families become one big family. The church acts to keep the families unified and bonded" (Interview 07149001). Another pastor expands on this theme and ties it into containment of suicide, which he refers to as "self-murder":

[Interview 07149003] We are interwoven, so to speak, into each family. We consider ourselves a family. That's all I teach, is family. I preach that when you join the church, you join the family of God, and we look upon one another as family. So what we do to keep that family alive is come to one another's rescue at all times. I guess that's what makes our families so strong. We don't just meet on Sundays like the white churches. We are the life blood, so to speak, of the black family. Our families can always come to us and not be ashamed to come to the church for help, prayer, or strength. We try to keep a family atmosphere. I guess we could say that this probably keeps our people in line. Especially when it comes to self-murder. We have such an outreach in our community that we always are in touch with our people. When you have somebody that cares about you like we do you don't have to give up on anything. We are one big family.

Other informants also stress the unity of family and church. They add that the emotional and spiritual needs of members are met by the church, and that the church serves to educate and inform its members in a way that strengthens the family. This view is articulated in a number of ways:

[Interview 07179003] We say so many times untruthfully that we are one big happy family. But we also know that in families there are problems. And yes, we are one big happy family here, but we do have

our problems. We have been able to work those problems out in a way that it mends those places that have been broken and it makes strong who we are as a people. The church is that institution which is able to keep a family together. It strengthens our relationships. It helps us learn to communicate and it does what no other institution can do. The church does . . . the church has been . . . the church will always be the only institution that has been a life-saving force in the black family's whole setup.

[Interview 10219024] We are the family. As we see the family, we are the body of Christ. The family is the church and that's how we see that.

[Interview 07149002] The Bible tells us what our role is to our families. That is where we go to deal with our families. We believe in the Word of God and are obedient to it. The role of the church is to keep the family together. The church is also there to educate, inform, and help as much as possible. That has always been the role of the black church throughout the ages. That's what has kept our people together.

[Interview 08269010] There is a statement that I love. The church is all we have and the church is all we need. The church is a family. We treat each other like a family. I said to my wife this morning, "I want our church to be the kind of church that a person that's not loved can be loved in." Our church is family.

In the pastors' view, the church has shaped the black family. This view is in agreement with the literature, which says that the church is firmly established as central in the black community. The church has been and continues to be the primary socializer, organizer, communicator, educator, and liberator of the black family.

This universal nature and function of the church serves to provide values, norms, attitudes, and beliefs essential to countering suicide in the black community. Further, the socially integrative effect of the church supports the notion that the church and the family are, in a sense, one entity.

Establishing the significance of the church in the community does not guarantee that the church's views on suicide are widespread in black culture. However, such significance is a necessary condition for the pervasiveness of these views, and the qualitative evidence of the study and of the literature establishes that this condition does exist. Therefore, a central objective of the study was to hear the pastors express their views, on the grounds that such views are not confined to the pastors' own personal opinions. Those views fit the hypothesis that religious norms shared in the black community counter suicide. The pastors condemn suicide and define it as so alien to the black experience that even contemplating suicide is alien to what it means to be African American.

THE CHURCH'S DEFINITION OF SUICIDE

The first aspect of suicide explored in the interviews was the pastors' definition of what constitutes suicide. Emile Durkheim defined suicide as "all cases of death resulting directly or indirectly from a positive or negative act of the victim himself, which he knows will produce this result" (Durkheim, 1951, p. 44). This definition is consistent with those given in the interviews. The concept of suicide generally is considered to be willful, premeditated, and not in accord with a sound judgment. The prevailing definition of suicide within the community is that suicide is a nonproductive act whereby a person takes his or her own life.

Although the views of the pastors jibe with those of Durkheim, there is a tendency to expand upon the definition to include other forms of self-injurious behavior, such as alcohol or drug use and "hanging out on the streets." Several pastors believe that a causal relationship exists between alcohol and drug use and suicide. While the clearest form of suicide, taking deliberate and immediate action to end one's life, is most condemned, some pastors expand the concept of suicide to refer to self-injurious behavior such as drug use, which could be a less clearly deliberate form of suicide. This attitude is evidenced in the following interview excerpts:

[Interview 08119007] Substance abuse is a form of suicide. It might be a slower form of suicide, but it's suicide. Once you start doing it, it's

suicide, and it's suicide. The finality of suicide is physical death, but suicide begins when you start doing substances, crack, cocaine, you know, marijuana. Those are smaller symptoms of suicide that lead up to the finality.

[Interview 08099006] Suicide includes drugs because when you look at our circumstances that we are faced with in our society, so many of our young people are really committing suicide through drugs.

The pastors were not asked direct questions about their views on and explanations of other forms of deviance in the black community as they were about suicide. However, a general reading of all thirty pastor interviews indicates essential agreement with these opinions. One pastor puts it very succinctly:

[Interview 07149002] Suicide is not doing the right thing. Suicide is hanging out there on these street corners selling dope, wasting your time doing nothing, drinking to death . . . ah . . . you know, all them things that are negative and serve the devil's will and not God's. All of these things are not of God. They poison the body, which is the temple of God. Suicide is more than pulling a trigger or cutting your wrist. Of course that would be suicide, too.

Some of the same sentiment is expressed by another church leader:

[Interview 07149001] Well, I believe that suicide is a person killing himself. Regardless of what way he do it. It makes no difference. When a person gives up on life be it with dope, alcohol or self-murder . . . that's all suicide.

As we shall see later, however, this fusing of suicide and other self-injurious acts is not maintained throughout by the pastors. Rather, they see a difference between clearly intended suicide and other actions such as taking drugs. Both are condemned, but deliberately and directly taking one's own life is seen as somehow less understandable and more unthinkable for black people.

CONDEMNATION OF SUICIDE

The case is clear: the pastors' view of suicide not only reflects their theological view of suicide, that is, that suicide is sinful and opposes God's authority, but underscores their political, economic, and social attitudes. Because suicide denies the sovereignty of God and is contrary to the teachings of the church, there is a consensus among pastors condemning the act.

The black community unequivocally condemns suicide as sin. The views of the interviewed pastors include the notion that "man is not the giver of life. Hence, man has not the authority to take life." In other words, "The Lord giveth and *only* the Lord taketh away." This attitude is evidenced in the following interview excerpts:

[Interview 07149002] Suicide is wrong. It is against God and nature. It's sinful and you cannot repent. Your soul is lost forever in hell.

[Interview 08119007] It's a serious sin. If a person don't have time to repent then they are in big trouble.

[Interview 08169008] We believe that suicide, or self-murder, is a sin that one cannot be forgiven for.

[Interview 08269010] We don't condone suicide. We condemn it to the maximum. We believe that most people that commit never ask for forgiveness.

[Interview 09229020] It is terrible. It's against God and God does not accept it and it is sin. After it is committed I fully believe definitely that there is no chance of forgiveness for it.

An additional perception that surfaces in the interviews is that blacks possess something uniquely and inherently black: a black "soul." The soul represents life in both a spiritual and worldly sense. The soul is tied to the black experience both culturally and traditionally. If one is to insure a proper place (i.e., heaven) for one's soul after death, it is important to live life as productively as possible. Obstacles encountered should not be a deterrent to live, but an encouragement to struggle.

To struggle with the help of God is believed to enhance the quality of life, making the individual resilient to pressures that otherwise would lead to suicide. Suicide does nothing for the soul except place it in peril of eternal damnation. The soul belongs to God and is entrusted to the individual, who is ultimately held accountable. It may be, then, that this norm of accountability for one's own life and soul is transmitted in both sacred and secular versions throughout the community.

Pastors were asked: "Has suicide ever been discussed from the pulpit? If so, what have you said?" Typical responses from those answering in the affirmative were as follows:

[Interview 09119017] Black people believe in a heaven and hell. We've been taught, as black people, that if you kill yourself you automatically goes to hell. There's no forgiveness for self-murder. This is true in thinking with the Bible. There's no forgiveness.

[Interview 07289001] God did not put us here to determine our own conclusion of life and taking it upon ourselves to make quick exits. That, biblically, is not an approved act of God. It's unpardonable sin. One who commits suicide goes to hell and is unpardoned for their sin.

[Interview 07179004] Well now, you know, according to the Bible, we have what we call heaven and hell. Christ Jesus came to make it possible that whosoever believeth in Him and follow His plan and is baptized, shall be saved. That's to escape eternal damnation. That's eternal separation from God. But a person who violates and rejects the promise and the plan of Jesus Christ, there is no other place for them but eternal separation from God. That's hell. What I try to do is get them to see the importance of accepting Christ. That's the first thing. To reject Christ is to just choose the way of eternal damnation, you see. To reject Christ means suicide to life in general. But to accept Christ is to accept everlasting life.

[Interview 09089015] If you take your own life, why, it's a lost cause not only this life but in the life to come. I feel like blacks really consider this even more so that they have a soul that they must give an account for.

The reasoning is clear: suicide is wrong because it is a denial of the sovereignty of God. The soul belongs to God and is entrusted to the individual who is held ultimately accountable. This accountability is transmitted to the community by the church, which puts a great value on life.

It should be noted here that only a few of the pastors have delivered sermons specifically on the topic of suicide. The primary reason for not doing so is that suicide is not seen as a problem in the black community. One pastor describes this view succinctly:

[Interview 09039011] Unlike crack, alcohol abuse, and crime, suicide is not a prevailing problem in the black community. Dealing with suicide is not an oversight, it just is not a problem. So why try to fix something if it is not broke?

THERE IS ALWAYS HOPE

In general, the church recognizes no reason for suicide. It allows no justification for giving up. Suicide is not for the true believer, a person who is "born again" or "saved." (Vignettes are identified by one letter and two numbers and are located in Appendix D. The letter and number refer to both the situation and situation number.)

[Interview 07149002, Vignette S1.1] If you are saved you don't have to take yourself out. As sick as I have been in my lifetime, I have never thought of killing myself. As a pastor, I visit my members in the hospital when they are sick. I have never been with any of my members . . . I mean they have had cancer of all types, kinds, shapes. Not one of them ever said that they wanted out of this here life. They always asked for prayer. Most of them wanted to live. They even prayed for healing. Some of them said that if it be God's will they would die. Saved folks believe in God and his healing power.

[Interview 09039011] Christ gives us purpose for living and therefore we want to live to the fullest and do all the good we can while we live. And no one wants to die soon anyway, but I think in the black community those who are religiously inclined, those who are members of the church, those who worship God tend to accept His value, the value that God places on life and therefore they are not prone to suicide.

Being a believer means accepting the authority and autonomy of God. This acceptance allows the individual to be shielded from or "not prone to suicide."

Even catastrophic illness is not a reason to kill oneself, when hope lies in prayer and healing. One pastor notes:

[Interview 08119007, Vignette S1.2] Suicide because of an illness is senseless. A person who know Jesus Christ . . . who understand who Jesus is and what he done for them . . . black or white they know that they have a high hope. The hope is not just in what we have here, but what we can accumulate here and how we do here. We got hope beyond this place.

From these statements it becomes increasingly evident that suicide is viewed as an act that stops the individual from fulfilling God's intention. Suicide simply is not God's will. As one pastor says:

[Interview 10289030] Suicide is the premature taking of one's own life by measures not consistent with a sound judgment. My theological view of suicide is that, as the scriptures say, "All things work to the good of all who love the Lord. They will be called according to his purpose." I feel that there is a purpose in everybody's life. Therefore, the taking of one's life is not within the framework of God's perfect will.

These views resonate in the black community's larger perception that suicide is never an acceptable answer. Everyone has a purpose in life, and the taking of one's life denies this purpose and challenges God's autonomy. While lashing out at hardship in other ways may make some sense or serve some purpose for certain individuals, suicide does not.

VIEWS ON THE CAUSES OF SUICIDE, AND
WHY THE SUICIDE RATE AMONG BLACKS
IS RELATIVELY LOW

The pastors were asked directly why they believed that suicide was less of a problem for the African-American community. In chapter 1, it was noted that the literature on black suicide expected that, in the absence of protective factors, blacks would attempt and complete suicide more frequently. I shall expand somewhat on that theme here as background for reporting the pastors' views on causes and prevention of suicide.

The absence of a role model in the black family leads us to the black family deficit theory. This theory attempts to explain suicide among black females and youths. The dual role of black females as sole wage earners and heads of households is hypothesized to maximize the propensity of suicide (Davis, 1979, 1980a, 1982). For black youths, the absence or loss of a "sensitive, strong, loving, masculine father figure causes psychological damage and leads to suicide" (Hendin, 1969, pp. 407–22).

Gibbs and Martin's (1971) status integration theory proposes that the rate of suicide, black or white, is inversely related to the degree of integration of the group to which one belongs (Durkheim, 1951). Status integration theory represents the conceptual framework most widely used to explain the higher suicide and suicide attempt rates among younger than among older blacks (Davis, 1980b, p. 226). Proponents of this theory argue that black suicide is premised on admission to the middle-class "American dream." That is, despite the social, political, and economic gains of the civil rights era, African Americans have not been able to overcome the many negative social forces inherent in their experience.

According to the theory, the fact that African Americans have been slow in transcending barriers in order to achieve a status comparable to or better than that of their white counterparts may be contributing to suicide, attempted suicide, and suicide ideations among African Americans. Others argue that the stresses associated with urbanization (i.e., poverty, discrimination, poor housing, low educational levels, and unemployment) act as an impetus to black suicide.

In this study, pastors offer two explanations for suicide and attempted suicide in the black community, each of which is consistent with these deprivation and deficit theories, as well as with Davis' proposition that suicide among African Americans is likely to occur with the weakening of the relational system (Davis, 1980b, p. 228). The first explanation attributes suicide to a breakdown in religious and family ties.

The second explanation suggests that suicide and attempted suicide among African Americans are related to the stress associated with the assimilative effects of racial integration. This greater integration into larger society is believed to undermine the internal integration and values of the black community. African Americans have assimilated materialistic values, beliefs, and mores of white culture, and these changes, along with weakening ties in the black community, induce a greater readiness to commit suicide.

According to the pastors, the effects of this process have been "devastating." This view is echoed in the following interviews:

[Interview 09049013] I think in this case it goes back to our culture. We have been taught down through the years that we as a people don't do these kinds of things so far as committing suicide. As a boy growing up I never knew anything about blacks committing suicide until integration came about and I believe black America then began to take on the traits, if you will, of white America.

[Interview 09229020] We as a race have always been used to hardships. We are more used to hardships than whites. Suicide was always more prevalent among whites than it was blacks. I personally believe that if black folks are killin' they self it's because of the integration. We've gotten where we're communicating closer with whites every day.

Violence, according to the pastors, is not an inherent part of African tradition. Each pastor boldly states that such violence has been transmitted to African Americans via racial integration. Such effects (black-on-black crime and drug abuse), according to the pastors, threaten the survival and development of African Americans. The question follows: Why don't these effects also make for high suicide rates among blacks?

SUICIDE IS A "WHITE THING"

Collectively, the pastors believe that while African Americans may have become violent, suicide is not a part of that violence and is not perceived as a social problem that has severe implications for the black community. The clear message is that suicide is a nearly complete denial of black identity and culture. Suicide is not in the black experience—it simply is not done. That suicide is a "white thing" underlies the concern that, as a result of racial integration, blacks may become more like whites in their suicidal behavior.

The perception that suicide is a "white thing" is prevalent in the black community. This deep-seated assumption was not initially a focus of this study, nor did any question in the interview schedule or survey allude to it as a "white thing." Suicide is viewed as peculiar to whites not simply because of its greater statistical frequency among whites, but because suicide is seen as inherent in white culture but almost totally antithetical to black culture. This notion was clearly communicated to me when several pastors insisted that I should know better than to ask questions about blacks and suicide because "suicide is a white thing." Their comments included: "As a rule, blacks don't kill themselves . . . you should know this already"; "Well, being black you should know that black people want to live"; "You should know that suicide is somethin' that occurs over there, on the other side of the tracks"; and "We want to live, son . . . we want to get there . . . you should know this."

This aversion to suicide is such an assumed part of being black that a black individual is surprised to hear the question, especially from another black. This assumption applies not only to religious people, but to all blacks. Even though the pastors and I were openly religious, and the topic at hand was religious beliefs on suicide, the pastors did not say: "You should know that, you're a Christian." They said: "You should know that, you're black."

The pastors interviewed for this study are unanimously of the opinion that the same difficulties and problems that lead to suicide among whites do not pose a threat to African Americans. This view is substantiated by the congregations surveyed. The belief is that economic, political, and social deprivation have made African Americans more resilient:

[Interview 07179003] The suicide rate being so low among blacks goes back to the strength that we have as a culture. It goes back to the value systems that we were taught and even having been taught those value systems. We never get away from them. We have always been aware of what our roles were. We have always been aware of what our strengths were. Our strengths have overpowered our weaknesses. That has made us bold up, brace our shoulders back, and stand firm. In a sense, allow the bullets to bounce off. The bullets hurt, but we've been taught to stand strong.

It should be noted that suicide is indeed condemned by whites, and the religious beliefs of white Christians regarding suicide probably differ little from the beliefs of black Christians. Yet, the significance of the church in the black community is believed to result in a stronger and more pervasive incorporation of those beliefs. This reference to Christian beliefs should not be taken to mean that other faiths adhered to by blacks, such as Islamic or Jewish faiths, would take a different stance on suicide. Non-Christian churches are found in few black communities, but in this community the only black churches are Christian.

The concept that whites and blacks are fundamentally different in their responses to stress is articulated clearly by the pastors. The black experience is seen as culturally, historically, politically, economically, and socially different from the white experience. Through their struggle, African Americans have developed an apparent resilience to behavior that otherwise would be self-destructive.

[Interview 07149002] It is a low-down shame for people to take their lives. That is something I could never quite understand. Uh . . . of course I don't know of a single negro that has committed suicide. That's just something our people don't do. I am from the South. Been here all my life. We grew up on the land with values. Nobody took from their neighbor and nobody took themselves out. That's just something we never heard of in our community. Uh . . . onlyes' time we ever heard about somebody killin' themselves was through rumors. Them rumors didn't even deal with negroes. They were all white folks. My mama and dad struggled all their life and their people before them struggled. None of them ever thought about killin' themselves. I have struggled uh . . . you know son . . . we been strugglin' all of our lives. The greater the sufferin' . . . you know . . . what we going to get will be better in heaven. That's what the ole time preachers said. That's what my people always said . . . uh . . . and so we always coped with whatever the deal was.

[Interview 07149001] As a rule they want to live. In my lifetime I have not witnessed a single black person that committed suicide. Well, one of the things is, you know, black people want to live. They want to live until they die. Most black people that are religious just believe that when God gets ready He's going to take away their life and they don't have to do it themselves. As a rule, the average person in the black community have to struggle to obtain everything he gets.

[Interview 07179003] I worked as a clinical counselor at Georgia Mental Health Institute for nine years, basically dealing with whites who were at that point of committing suicide. There were very few blacks there because of that reason. The institution had very few blacks there period. One of the things that I have noticed as I've worked with them in counseling is that blacks have been faced with struggles and stresses all of their lives. It's something that they have endured through slavery and blacks have learned how to handle those pressures which does not allow them to even commit or attempt suicide. Nine times out of ten you find whites wanting to take their life. On the other hand, my Afro-American

brothers and sisters have either worked through those issues or found ways out that were healthy.

[Interview 0714900l] Like with white folks, it would be materialism causing them to kill themselves. Not being able to deal with things they struggled hard to get being taken away from them.

[Interview 09179018] White people are a little different than black. White people will give up quick under certain circumstances. White boys will kill their self over a girl. Girls will kill their self over boys. Blacks won't do that. Blacks will say, "Well, the heck with that. There's another one out there somewhere." They'll use the term "she's not the only fish in the sea" and go on. Whites, if they lose something or somebody, they'll commit suicide over it. A black won't.

[Interview 08099006] Well, on suicide, as I look at it, in the white race, seemly' they—their views on life is different from the black American, and seemly' if they are not able to carry out their objectives in life, to me, they gets in a more pressure stage, and they're certain to commit suicide more fastly, to my belief.

The pastors portray blacks as being more religious, as a group, than their white counterparts. Additionally, blacks are described as being able to endure more hardships without succumbing to the despair and despondency that lead to suicide.

The black experience in America is one of struggle. Life in the black community is a struggle. Survival represents hope and the promise of a better life after death. The church unifies African Americans around a common tradition shaped out of suffering. It is the church that offers strength, identity, coping skills, and a reason for living. Thus, suicide is excluded as contradictory to what it means to be black. Whites may do it, but blacks do not.

SUMMARY

Pastors share the view that the church is intrinsic to the nature and development of the black culture. The aspirations of African

Americans are linked to a struggle that is an outgrowth of the church. The church has a unique place in the black community. It provides social integration and it instills in African Americans attitudes, values, beliefs, and mores that counter suicide. The church leaders interviewed in this study point to the black church as an institution that has provided structural, demographic, and cultural integration, and that has not only sustained hope for African Americans, but has provided resiliency in the face of deprivation.

An extension of the black family, the church is the institution in which African Americans are socialized. In fact, the black church and family are so inseparable that the church sets the standards by which the black family functions.

Religious norms pervasive in the black community overwhelmingly condemn suicide. Suicide is perceived as sinful and as "against God's perfect will." A distinction is seen between "clearcut" suicide and other self-injurious behavior such as drug abuse. While both behaviors are deplored, clear-cut suicide is more unthinkable than other self-injurious acts.

For the most part, African Americans in this study attribute any suicide to the assimilative effects of integration and to the disintegration of religious interests and family bonds. Suicide is not perceived as being part of the black identity. It is, however, associated with being white: it occurs in white America, or "across the tracks." African Americans may express violence outwardly, but, in the words of one pastor, "to our credit, at least we don't kill ourselves."

The next chapter will present, through discussion of vignettes, a clearer picture of church leaders' attitudes, opinions, and beliefs concerning suicide as opposed to other forms of self-injurious and deviant behavior. The goal of the vignettes is to contrast responses to suicide with those to more prevalent forms of deviance, such as crime and alcohol and drug abuse in the black community. It is then possible to compare the perceived roles that the black church and family play in these social issues.

Chapter 3

Black Suicide, Drugs, and Crime

Part of an understanding of the social meaning of suicide in the black community comes from our knowledge of the norms and social relations of the black church and family. The literature suggests that the black church and the black family have influenced the low rates of suicide within the black community. However, these institutions appear to have been less effective in countering violence among blacks.

Through the use of vignettes, this chapter examines suicide and other forms of life-threatening behavior. In presenting the findings from the vignettes, responses are identified by notations such as [Interview 07149002, Vignette S1.1]. The first eight numbers in this notation indicate the interview date and number. Vignette S1 indicates a response to the first vignette, that is, Situation 1; Vignette S1.1 indicates a response to the first vignette, question one. The vignettes can be found in appendix D.

This study offers no comparison between black religious views on suicide and white attitudes toward suicide. While the pastors frequently offer comparisons based on their experiences (these are reported), it was felt that the effect of religious views on suicide needed to be examined in some additional way. This examination is the purpose of the vignettes. They are utilized to compare the effect of the church on suicide with the role of the church regarding other forms of deviance. The vignettes depict different situations and behavior regarding suicide, crime, and drugs. Informants were asked to respond to each scenario. Their responses have been examined to discover differences, if any, between the normative climates for suicide and for other forms of deviance.

The initial intent of the study was to review responses to real cases of suicide, but preliminary inquiries showed little chance of doing so, as no cases were found among the informants' congregations. The first vignette presents a hypothetical scenario that involves a suicide and the second depicts a hypothetical attempted suicide. The other two vignettes present hypothetical situations involving violence and drugs.

The first vignette describes a situation in which a suicide had occurred:

> A church mother, whom you have known for years, has changed since her husband of forty years committed suicide after learning that he had prostate cancer. She stays relatively to herself, has dropped out of church activities, lost weight, and appears unkempt. At first you thought that her behavior was typical of mourning, but it has now been well over a year since her husband's demise and she appears to be getting worse instead of better.

The pastors were asked seven follow-up questions (see appendix D). For instance: "What would you say about her husband's suicide?" This question was asked both to elicit additional information on attitudes, values, and norms and to elicit social responses to members in whose family a suicide had occurred.

In response, the pastors articulate a viewpoint that is supportive and caring toward the widow, but offer strong opposition to suicide and absolutely no justification for the taking of one's life. Again, a clear distinction is drawn between the way in which African Americans would react to the situation and the way in which they believe whites would react. Typical responses include:

[Interview 07149002, Vignette S1.1] Sin. He probably wasn't saved. If he had been saved, he probably would not have taken himself out. If you are saved son you would know what I am talking about. Saved folk

believe in God and his healing power. This is an interesting situation. As sick as I have been in my lifetime, I have never thought of killing myself. As a pastor, I visit my members in the hospital when they are sick. I have never been with any of my members . . . I mean they have had cancer of all types, kinds, shapes and uh . . . not one of them ever said that they wanted out of this here life. They always asked for prayer. Most of them wanted to live . . . even prayed for healing . . . uh . . . some of them said that if it be God's will they would die. So this here is not typical of a black person with a sickness. Now I have known and heard of white folks in this position killing themselves.

[Interview 08119007, Vignette S1.1] The power that Jesus have left us through divine healing, what's already provided for us in atonement, he didn't have to commit suicide.

[Interview 08099006, Vignette S1.1] First of all, he committed a sin that should not have been committed. Because the Lord said thou shall not kill, and just he had a disease that mostly he felt within himself was incurable. That doesn't mean that he should've taken his own life. Personally, he made a very bad mistake. Because, the Bible really say in 130 Psalms, the Lord said he forgiveth thy iniquities and he healeth all thy diseases. So many times the Lord allows different trials to come upon his people in various places. That could have been one of his trials to see whether he could . . . whether he could remain steadfast in the face of that.

[Interview 10279025, Vignette S1.1] Well, as far as her husband's suicide, I would say that he lost the hope that is ingrained or that I try to, as pastor, instill in all of my parishoners, particularly that there is hope. Life is a empty vessel without a certain amount of hope. That's the reason, I would think, that the incident lead to suicide. The hope in our lives, it has a tendency to sustain us. As dark, as bleak as life may be at whatever point, when there is a ray of hope one seems to be able to mount whatever opposition or problem he or she is going through with and looking for a brighter and a better day.

The overall condemnation of suicide as sin remains clear. Terminal or painful disease is no excuse for giving up. It merely enhances the quality of life through struggle. After all, struggling is inherently part of the black experience.

The pastors have many views concerning what constitutes suicide. When asked "How do you define the husband's suicide?" the pastors respond in the following manner:

[Interview 0903011, Vignette S1.2] I would define the suicide in this case as being one that has resulted because of a lack of faith; the lack of trust in God. The physical illness has caused them to give up faith and trust. I would define it as a loss of faith and lack of trust in God.

[Interview 09119017, Vignette S1.2] You kill yourself and you think you're out of the trouble. You're really tormenting the flames. No way to be saved when you kill yourself. So, now, if a man commits suicide, you know he's going to hell. It's a written thing. He's bound for hell. Ain't no chance to forgive, to get forgiveness because you don't have no chance to ask for forgiveness.

[Interview 09229019, Vignette S1.2] I'd define it as an act of foolishness. Because there is a God above and he say, "Anything you ask in my name, I'll give it to you." But, he didn't ask to heal him; he didn't ask God to put him on the right direction to get healed.

[Interview 09269021, Vignette S1.2] I would define it as, as a suicide where unfortunately, the person just lost hope, gave up hope. But I think that if perhaps someone could have, again a family member or someone that's real strong, could've just continued to encourage his heart to hold on or to hang in there, this could've been prevented.

[Interview 08269010, Vignette S1.2] I would define that as being a problem that he did not really know the Lord. He never trusted the Lord. People brought up in the church don't commit suicide. They're hooked on the fact that even to death God is gonna take care of it. It's gonna change. It's gonna get better. The Lord is gonna see to it.

[Interview 08099006, Vignette S1.2] I would define his suicide as very, very disrespectful to the Lord as his servant, because if he had been a child of God and trusting in the Lord, then after a period of years, he

should've known—he knew that anyway, that it was wrong to destroy his own life.

[Interview 07149002, Vignette S1.2] It is just like I said . . . sinful! We would just have to pray for his soul. I can't pass judgment on this here man. I don't know what was going on in his mind. I can only say that whatever it was . . . uh . . . he didn't take it to the altar. That's where he should have gone. I believe we could have saved him and given him that peace he needed. Now, he will never have that peace.

The pastors continue to express the belief that there is always hope. This hope is premised on faith in God's healing power, which serves to sustain life and shield the individual from self-destruction.

Suicide is viewed as that which destroys the soul, rebukes God's omnipotence, and deters one from reaching one's true potential and fulfilling God's will. Given the centrality of the church and its moral leadership, these religious views most likely permeate black America and transmit to the black community that suicide is never an acceptable remedy. These views on suicide may not be held as strongly by the community as they are by these pastors, but they can be expected to be shared to a large extent.

The next chapter will demonstrate that these views are indeed shared by church members. While this study cannot determine how widespread such beliefs are outside the church, the pastors clearly feel that their moral authority goes beyond the church to exceed that of other community leaders. According to some pastors:

[Interview 07289005, Vignette S1.3] It would vary. It depends on the pastor. The black church has always moved according to the pastor.

[Interview 08269010, Vignette S1.3] In the black church the people look at the minister and the response of the minister usually flows through the congregation. I mean 99 percent of the church goes the way that the minister goes and it is very different from a white church. Very different, very different. The minister in the black community is the power. That's the source. It's not the schoolteacher or the judge. It's the black minister.

So the congregation is going to respond how the minister is. In fact, they wait on a word from the minister about the situation and then they will come back repeating what the minister said about the situation. So if the minister tells the church, "The Lord is gonna fix it for mother," then the church will start saying to one another, "The Lord is gonna fix it."

The view that the ministers influence active church participants and others is echoed in the interview protocols of other pastors, further supporting the notion that the church influences much of what happens within the black community.

African Americans view themselves as being more religious, more spiritual than their white counterparts, and more able to endure hardships. This attitude is reflected in the interviews, survey, and vignette responses. For instance, pastors were asked, "Suppose you could have encountered her husband before his suicide?" Typical responses underscore the importance of having a strong connection to the church, faith in the authority of God, and strong, loving support from church, family, and friends:

[Interview 08299009, Vignette S1.7] I would have dealt with him through scriptures and continued to give him scriptures that even when the doctors have given up on him there is hope. If he would have the faith, God could perform a miracle. He should trust God regardless because God could be able to perform a miracle in his life. If he was white it probably would have happened much quicker. I just think the white person would have given up easier because he probably wouldn't have had that faith in God to trust as long.

[Interview 07149002, Vignette S1.7] Well, knowing that he had cancer I would have been visiting with him on a regular basis. I do this with all my members that are sick. I would be praying with him—the word of God is powerful enough to keep him from killing himself. You know, the word of God—God's grace—yes—glory is powerful enough to heal him. It saved my soul and made me whole. Understand what I am talking about? That's what I would have done. Together with his wife and church family we would have that shield—that armor to protect him. I am talking about the church family. The church is our mother . . . uh . . . shield—our

only hope. That's what has always been there when it looked like we were lost. With God and the church . . . uh . . . this man would have gone to glory if it had been God's will. Not any time sooner.

[Interview 07179004, Vignette S1.7] I would encourage him that the same God that worked miracles in the past is still interested in his survival and suicide is not the answer: God give you life and you're still living. Live with what you have under the fear and direction of the Lord, and let Him, when He gets ready—if you take your life Brother Jones, then how do you know that God did not have a plan to heal you, or maybe God will use you through a ministry even with what you're living with. Others have had cancer and they was healed Brother Jones, and therefore, if you're going to take it into your own hands, that's not wise. The scriptures teaches that we're not to be wise of our own conceit, but to trust in the Lord with all our heart and lean not unto our own understanding. In all our ways, acknowledge Him, Brother Jones, and He shall direct your path. Will you accept His Word? Accept his Word, Brother Jones. This is not the way. I love you. God love you. Your family love you. This church love you. You got friends that's been around you. You're not alone. Brother Jones, God loves you and he does not want you to take matters in your own hands. Think about it. This body that you live in is not really you. You didn't make this body. You didn't create this body. That's God. Brother Jones, as your brother, as your pastor, and as a Christian, try to stand before God with a natural cause of death and not suicide."

[Interview 09119017, Vignette S1.7] Well, if I could have talked to him I would have told him that you don't need to take your own life. The Lord give you your life. You ought to stay here long as you can. When the Lord get ready for you, He'll come get you. He'll take your life from you when He get ready. But you don't need to rush it off and end your life because of some kind of exciting news you got and all like that. I'd tell him, no, you don't need to do that. If you put your trust in God and faith in Him and read your Bible, why, this will help you tide over the problems that you have.

Among African Americans, faith and reliance upon God and family are seen as the factors that influence the individual's ability to struggle against and to withstand elements that contribute to suicide among other racial and ethnic groups.

Through religious expression, the African American traditionally and historically has been able to find refuge from political, economic, and social oppression and from hardship during illness. The social integration factors in operation here lie in the black family and church, both of which have shown resiliency under stressful conditions. The responses here allow no justification for suicide. Even under the most traumatic conditions, suicide is unthinkable and unimaginable.

To further investigate views on suicide and responses to suicidal behavior, the second vignette contained a situation involving an attempted suicide:

> A fifteen-year-old boy has reacted badly to his parent's divorce some months ago. Always extroverted, the child is now quiet and withdrawn. In school the child isolates himself from his peers and has dropped off the basketball team. His friends avoid him and his grades have dropped. His father was always active in his life, and you suspect that he feels abandoned by him. His mother, with whom he lives, tends to let him alone to do whatever he wants. The child has told a school counselor that he is tired of living and that he would like to go to a faraway, problem-free place where he can find ultimate peace. The child insists that he is the reason that his parents aren't living together. He believes that the divorce would not have occurred if his parents really loved him. Frustrated, the child has come to you to tell you of his attempts to find a way to escape from it all. Crying and rolling up his sleeves slowly, the child reveals scars where he has slashed his wrists several times.

The pastors were asked four follow-up questions in order to determine their perception of suicide attempts (see appendix D). For example: "Talk to me like you would talk to that boy regarding suicide," and "How would you as a pastor approach this boy's mentioning of suicide?"

From the following excerpts we see that even attempted suicide is viewed as unimaginable, and is as widely condemned as completed suicide. Again, the response to attempted suicide is caring and supportive, but the attempt is condemned as a sin that will bring eternal judgment.

[Interview 10279025, Vignette S2.1] I would not have let it get to the point where the youth was ready to end his life. I think one of the key things, as a pastor, is for the pastor to be aware of the behavior of his members, particularly in a church where the membership is not up in the hundreds. It provides the pastor a bit more personal relations, more personal contact with members of his congregation. Secondly, the child, as a result of the divorce, felt that he has lost a great deal. Life was not worthy of being continued by him and so he sought to end his life by various means. I would try to make him feel in view of the fact that his father and mother has divorced, I would, to some degree, fill that void as a father since I am the pastor of the church and in many instances the father of the members of the church. I would try to make him feel comfortable in view of the fact that he has a substitute, that he has another male image that he can look up to, that he can feel proud of, that he can idolize, even though I will not be his father, but I could try to fill the void.

[Interview 09229019, Vignette S2.2] What would I tell you about killing yourself? I say, "Let me tell you something, son. If you kill yourself, that's not going to help mother nor father. Say, if you kill yourself, when time come to give an account of the deeds in your body, mother, father, sister, brother, and none other is going to stand before the judge but you. Say all of this will be up against you."

[Interview 09089015, Vignette S2.2] I'm gonna say "What would you gain by committing suicide? I mean, what would you get out of it? I mean, and most of all, are you ready to meet God? And what of your future? Do you plan to play basketball or football or tennis or golf or what have you? If you blot out your life now, you're going to lose it all. You're looking forward to the future with kids or a family. I mean, what is the profit of man even if he gain the whole world and lose his own soul? You commit suicide now, you gonna lose it all. So, I mean, from my standpoint, I've had situations in life and even in my early years, I can remember when I didn't have sufficient clothes to wear, shoes to wear, didn't have the food that I really would have liked to have eaten, but I

made it through. There are other sources that you can really go to get help. I mean, but if you take you life now, you're going to lose everything. You won't even have a chance to experience what's in store for you. I want you to know that you are not alone. I mean, I am here and I've had many experiences with young people and, you know, you can make it but if you give up on life now, there is no chance because there is no opportunity after you've gone to the grave."

[Interview 09039011, Vignette S2.2] I would say, "It's no need to kill yourself. Hey, they love you. Other people love you. You . . . getting along fine with your schoolmates. To take your life at the age of fifteen, with a lot of life ahead of you and a lot of things to do, a lot of achievements to make, get your degree, get your profession going, marry, have your family, got a lot going for you, so taking your life and ending it all is not the answer by no means. You can overcome this. Having a biblical foundation gives meaning and purpose for our lives. So all in all, no matter what, the expression in the black community with a strong religious background you say you believe and have value laid on life. It is good to be alive and to have purpose in our living. We are not just here like an animal or a plant in the forest; we have a purpose. We were created in the image of God and consequently you have a reason to live. Come on now, your parents love you. I love you. The church loves you."

[Interview 08299009, Vignette S2.2] I would let him know that life is really worth living and there is happiness and that he would make a great mistake if he would commit suicide because he has too much to live for. He has too much before him and certainly I would tell him that the Lord is there for him and if he would really seek God there is an answer to your problem and there is happiness with God and you can live on.

[Interview 08299009, Vignette S2.3] I would tell him that this is really not the right thing to do. We're not supposed to take our own lives because Jesus came that we might have life and that we might have it more abundantly. Jesus didn't come for us to commit suicide but he came that we might live.

[Interview 0809906, Vignette S2.3] As he would mention suicide, I would begin to inform him that, first of all, that is the wrong direction to

take. I would try to—I would say, "If you would try to, or destroy your life then, you could possibly wind up in hell, and nobody wants to go to that place. You as a young man, you got too much to look forward to. You're still in school possibly in junior high school. You don't know, you might become a doctor. You might become a lawyer. You might become a minister. Give life a chance. Get that thought out of your mind completely. If you allow the things I'm saying to you to become part of you, I guarantee you'll be a better person."

The interplay between church and family support the pervasive notion in the black community that there is always hope and that suicide is never an acceptable alternative. Each individual has a purpose in life. Hardship, difficulty, and injustice are no excuse—giving up through suicide is immoral and throws away any chance the individual has to reach his or her potential.

To investigate views on drug use, pastors were presented a third vignette (see appendix D), which described the behavior of a substance abuser:

> Ernest is a twenty-eight year old, single, unemployed man who has a problem with alcohol and multiple drug abuse (marijuana, Quaaludes, and crack). Ernest grew up in the church. He was baptized, sang in the youth choir, and always attended Sunday school and church services with his family. His family is still an active part of your congregation. Ernest, on the other hand, spends most of his time drinking very heavily with only several short periods of being sober. Ernest is still living at home with his parents. According to his mother, he comes and goes as he pleases. Ernest has been arrested several times by the local police and his driver's license was suspended over a year ago for driving while intoxicated. When Ernest is sober he makes an occasional appearance in church. However, when he is "high," he gets together with his old friends who, like him, misuse alcohol and drugs. Ernest needs help and his parents have asked you to intervene.

Pastors agree that the experience of African Americans in the United States has been saturated with violence. According to those interviewed, this problem has been magnified and perpetuated by the involvement of African Americans with alcohol and drugs.

The responses to questions such as, "How would you evaluate the seriousness of the situation and what would you do about it?" and "How would you evaluate Ernest's behavior?" show that church leaders perceive alcohol and substance abuse as a social problem that has severe implications in the black community. Unlike suicide and suicide attempts, the pastors report frequent experiences with persons involved in alcohol and drug abuse.

[Interview 08099006, Vignette S3.1] Now this young man is twenty-eight years old. He's single. He's without employment and he has taken a habit of drinking, using various drugs, and his family members are members of the same church. I would take it very seriously, because really I have been faced with situations basically on that same nature. I have even been to a seminar in Rochester, New York, especially on ways how to try to help persons that are involved in drinking and drugs. Because as we know, that is what is causing so many of our black young men to be destroyed today.

[Interview 07149002, Vignette S3.1] This is typical in the black family. Our families are different from white families . . . 'cause . . . like you see here, a twenty-eight year old still at home. I don't believe you have that with white families. They would have had that boy in some high-class, expensive place where he could get help. Us folk don't have that kind of money where we can provide that kind of care. All we have is the church. The church is always there. We do it all and take care of it all. This is uh . . . a serious problem in this picture.

[Interview 07149002, Vignette S3.2] Son, let me tell you. This behavior is bad business. It's typical of what is happening to our black men. I preach against this all the time. With the black family losing some of its power 'cause of all these material things uh . . . you know, fancy cars, jewelry, expensive homes, luxuries . . . uh . . . we never had these things and we lived our lives right. Now, the more our people, especially the young ones go for it . . . uh, this is where it takes them. What more can I say? Ernest's behavior is not right, but it's what's happening out there in the world.

[Interview 06129001, Vignette S3.1] Of course alcohol and drug abuse is a major problem. Here you have a twenty-eight year old, single, unemployed male still living at home with his parents. Probably the influence of his friends—they have more influence on him than probably his family has over him. Pretty much to evaluate the seriousness of the situation, I am not real sure whether I uh . . . well, doing what he is doing is wrong and . . . uh . . . but that's a good one because I am dealing with that particular issue right now in the community where we are. Unless we change the environment, change the demand for what he is doing he knows is wrong then we are not going to the person.

[Interview 09119017, Vignette S3.2] I was saying that the system is not set up where they actually help the poor people or black people as they claim they is supposed to help them. I don't think you do a man much good to give him an appointment to come back ten days later especially when he has told you "I need some help. Help me." And, I know I done prayed for him and all. I got a young man comes right here now. He comes to my house and he talks kind of around them and like and say he knows the Lord has got something for him to do and he's trying to get to it. I take hold of his hand and pray for him and goes on, but he still deals with that stuff. I say, "Son, are you still smoking that stuff?" And he says: "Reverend, I ain't gonna tell you no lie. I'm still smoking every once in a while." And whenever you got people like that, they really need professional help. I think they're short of people to work on people who are low-income when they get problems because I have known some of them to come through by getting professional help.

Note the contrast between the responses to this case and to the suicide vignettes. Interesting here is the fact that the pastors deplore the use of alcohol and drugs as a remedy for problems—they condemn substance abuse almost as much as suicide. But alcohol and drug use is not condemned to the degree to which suicide and other forms of deviance are condemned—rather, pastors are more sympathetic to how conditions might move one to crime and drugs.

In this case, Ernest's behavior is unacceptable, but understandable because of social conditions (i.e., unemployment, poverty, and lack of education) that can lead to deviant behavior. This viewpoint is articulated through comments such as: "Messin' with drugs is bad business and is a kind of suicide, but times being the way they are—no jobs and all—are killin' our young black men"; "There is no excuse for this here young man hanging out there doin' drugs, but what can someone who don't have an education and a job do?"; "A little boy told me that he could make more money selling dope than he could raking yards"; and "It's sin, but who is going to work for minimum wage when they can make one hundred times that much standin' on a corner lookin' out for the man?"

This attitude that substance use or abuse is unacceptable but understandable permeates the pastors' responses. It is helpful in explaining how the church's normative influence may aid in keeping the suicide rate low while it has less impact on other life-threatening behavior. The church may be able firmly to transmit values that serve to control and regulate self-destructive behavior; its uncompromising uniformity makes suicide unthinkable for most African Americans. On the other hand, the church's flexibility or "exception-to-the-rule" attitude apparently has little positive impact on other forms of life-threatening behavior. Drug abuse and violence against others are wrong, but not unthinkable.

The fourth situation (see appendix D) involves an young man who was recently arrested and charged with a murder, and who has a history of crime:

> Charles is an eighteen year old man who has just been arrested and charged with the murder of another young person. Charles grew up in the black community of Gainesville where he lived with his mother, a member of your church, and five siblings. Charles never knew his father, as his father abandoned his mother when Charles was an infant. As the oldest of six children, Charles spent most of his time caring for his younger brothers and sisters while his mother worked as a janitor in a downtown bank. Charles was an average student in high school until he dropped out in his junior year. He claims he dropped out of school for good reasons. Frustrated,

Charles began acting out at home and stealing from his mother's purse. Finally, Charles' mother told him to either get a job or go back to school where he could get his diploma. Unable to get a job, Charles got involved in law violations.

The pastors were asked four follow-up questions, including: "How would you evaluate Charles' behavior?" and "How would you evaluate the seriousness of Charles' situation?"

The pastors are unanimous in condemning the behavior, but offer possible explanations as to why Charles may have engaged in it. Recall that the pastors also vehemently oppose suicide, but allow no justification or rationale for the taking of one's life. They spend much time debating the issues that motivated Charles to commit murder, but will not consider these same issues as motivators for suicide. Typical responses to the fourth vignette are:

[Interview 07149001, Vignette S4.1] I would say that Charles' behavior was motivated by his parents. In other words, his parent in this case has the responsibility of disciplining and motivating. The mother with the six children—we could say the boy was very devoted to his family and he did all he could for his siblings. However, after he grew up to a certain age he began to feel smothered, so to speak, with responsibilities that he didn't earn. Many times it is wrong for the parents to put this type of responsibility on their children. This is the case for black Americans. My mother and father separated when I was six months old and I didn't see my father until I was six or eight years old. Eventually he died when I was twelve. So then the larger children had to take care of and maintain the responsibility as is typical of the black family. When the parent smothers the older child with the responsibility that he don't need or what he shouldn't have it always makes them find a way to get out. For instance, he don't have any money, no time, uh . . . the parents fail to appreciate him . . . uh . . . what I mean by appreciation—say something like, "You are doing a good job" or "You handled that situation well," etc. Our parents fail to do this. That leaves the child with nothing in terms of support. The child is then forced to find his own relief.

[Interview 07149002, Vignette S4.1] OK. This behavior is unacceptable, son. It seems to be what we are seeing more and more of in our

community. Parents not being responsible and placing what would be for them to do on their children. Our situation as a race has created this kind of thing . . . uh . . . our people don't have the kind of money white folks have to send our children to day care. We don't have the clubs and parks for our kids. So, our kids are left at home to grow up. This is what has happened to Charles. His behavior is typical of what we have been hearing about. That's why it is so important for the church to assist these mothers and fathers with their families.

[Interview 07149001, Vignette S4.2] Well, let's see . . . uh . . . it's pretty serious. The boy doesn't have any way of expressing his self other than the way you have it. That's what is happening to our children. They need to have right-of-way to the same things the white kids have. This would release some of the pressure on our mothers and fathers. Perhaps this would even keep our men and women from breaking up. It's serious son. A lot of these here families break up because there are too many pressures at home . . . ah . . . too many children, no jobs, no education and it goes on and on. Our families just don't have it easy like the white families. This causes our people to be frustrated and eventually they explode. Who else can they hurt but themselfs son. You know the story. The white man has so much control that they don't dare to hurt him. They are afraid to kill themselves so they go out and kill a brother. That's how it has always been. You can see this happening to Charles. He is so frustrated with what he doesn't have that he goes out and takes it. He's not taking it from the white man. He's taking it from his own. What can I say?

[Interview 09039011, Vignette S4.1] As always, people's response or reactions have some basis in the deficiency or lack of something that people want. In the case of Charles, an eighteen-year-old boy, perhaps he is frustrated never having known his father in the first place. The mother then is a single parent working to take care of them. He is given the ultimatum of going to school or get a job. Without education he can't get the job he want. So he ends up taking less of an approach in trying to steal rather than working and that leads on to the ultimate murdering somebody. So Charles' problem may be in the lack of self-esteem, beginning with frustration of not being able to get what he want and not having had any principles instilled in him by a father. Perhaps, he tried to take the less of ways to get on in life by stealing

and end up getting riotous or whatever and out of frustration or whatever ends up killing somebody. Maybe not premeditated, but kill somebody nevertheless. Now I don't know what that evaluation is viable or not but that is why I would look at it initially. By no means is it justifiable. I am trying to say that perhaps the root of his behavior is a combination of a lot of things. A lot of ramifications if you will. I am trying to show how some things can lead up to, way back there, not having had any parental guidance say from a father. Maybe the mother don't have even that much time anyway to be with him and he stuck with trying to rear his own brothers and sisters that are younger than him. No high school training and no job. The man is frustrated, perhaps feeling inferior and different from the other guys who got what he wants and he can't get it because he's not up to par.

[Interview 09049013, Vignette S4.2] I think Charles is no different from no other young man. He has allowed himself to get caught up in society. He wants what society has to offer him. He wants fastness. He wants quickness. He wants a quick dollar here and there. So he no longer wants to go to school. He says that he can't find a job. So what I'm gonna do is stay at home. I'm gonna steal everything that I can from my mom.

As reported by the pastors, there is no doubt that the black church condemns the use of alcohol and drugs, but note that there is a subtle shift from the way in which suicide is condemned. This shift does not seem to be in the degree to which suicide and drug abuse are condemned, rather, it appears to be the extent to which there are references to conditions or uncontrollable factors that may move one to crime and drugs. The behavior is unacceptable, but understandable because of the system and social conditions, unemployment, lack of education, influence of friends, and so on. "Messin' with drugs is bad business and is a kind of suicide, but times being the way they are—no jobs and all—are killin' our young black men." "There is no excuse for this here young men hanging out there doin' drugs, but what can someone who don't have an education and a job do?" "It's a sin, but who is going to work for minimum wage when they can make one hundred times that much standin' on a corner lookin' out for the man?"

This same perceptual shading is evident in the assessment given of the vignette depicting a homicide by a youngster with a history of crime (see appendix D). The pastors were unanimous in condemning the behavior and viewing it as extremely serious, but as with the case of drug abuse, they tended to offer plausible explanations of it.

For the most part, the pastors' view of crime and murder equals their view of suicide: they are sins. However, the pastors tend to see Charles as a victim of his environment. First, they blame the parents, insisting that black parents should not place their children in adult roles before the children reach adulthood. Second, they blame society for economic deprivation and not for providing black families with the benefits that are afforded to white families. Third, they insist that violence would be less prevalent in the black community if African Americans had better economic, educational, and employment opportunities.

Recall that in their responses to the suicide vignettes, the pastors refer to none of those circumstances. Suicide is sinful and adversity can be overcome without resorting to suicide. The pastors neither excuse nor justify violent behavior against others, but they do see it as explicable in the face of deprivation. They see suicide as inexplicable in the face of the same deprivation.

SUMMARY

Responses to the vignettes show a consensus among the pastors, and a consistency with the results of the first part of the interviews. The views of the pastors do not change, even in response to hypothetical situations involving suicide, attempted suicide, drug abuse, and crime. The pastors continue to emphasize that the church is firmly embedded in the black experience. Moreover, the pastors articulate their condemnation of and opposition to suicide, even as an escape from the pain of terminal illness. While they condemn crime and drug abuse, they somehow understand the behavior. For the most part, the pastors attribute violence in the black community to the "system," or to conditions (economic, political, and social) that provoke violence toward others, but not toward one's self. The church simply rejects suicide.

The next chapter will present the findings from congregation survey. The goal of the congregation survey was to measure the extent to which the views of the pastors have been transmitted to and are shared by the church members. The findings substantiate and partially validate information from the interviews with pastors.

Chapter 4

Survey of Church Members

Recall that the interviews with church pastors were conducted to learn the extent to which the African-American church constructs, transmits, and reinforces attitudes, values, beliefs, and norms that counter suicide in the African-American community. A part of the interviews utilized vignettes in order to compare and contrast the responses to norms concerning suicide with those regarding other forms of life-threatening behavior, such as alcohol and drug abuse and violent crime. The interview results were presented in chapters 2 and 3. This chapter will discuss the survey results.

The moral and social views promulgated by the church leaders and adhered to by active church participants should be influential in the views of the black community. While no attempt is made to demonstrate this influence in the community studied, the assumption of the centrality of the black church is common in the literature, is stated unequivocally by the pastors, and is shared, to a large extent, by church participants.

The percentage distribution of responses to key items in the questionnaire is presented in Tables 4.1 and 4.2. The original intention was to categorize responses according to a traditional Likert Scale (i.e., 1 = strongly disagree and 5 = strongly agree, with the midpoint indicating no opinion), but the concern was the degree of consensus among the congregations rather than the extent of disagreement. The responses essentially form a five-point ordinal scale of agreement or consensus, with 1 indicating no agreement and 5 the highest level of agreement.

The survey instructions (see appendix E) were given orally, after questionnaires had been distributed to each member present. Members were asked to express the extent of their agreement with each statement. Questions such as, "I don't understand these numbers all too well. What do they mean?" and "Can we circle more than one number?" were asked repeatedly, indicating confusion.

After several queries from members of the first church surveyed, respondents were instructed to "circle 1 if you disagree with the statement and one of the other four numbers if you agree with the statement." The intent was to anchor the responses to 1 on the scale. Unfortunately, no mechanism was provided for respondents to indicate "no opinion." For the sake of consistency, however, surveys were administered in the same manner to all remaining church groups. These flaws create a limit on the interpretation of the findings. However, it is reasonable to treat the responses as ordinal degrees of consensus, and that is how they will be treated in this analysis.

Tables 4.1 and 4.2 show the percentage distribution of responses to only ten of the seventeen statements in the questionnaire. Appendix G contains demographic data, as well as responses to all of the questionnaire items. The data in these tables indicate a high degree of consensus among the church members: their beliefs about suicide and other life-threatening and criminal behavior reflect the views held by the pastors.

Pastors were asked, "What is the role of the black church in the black community?" and "Is the black church a vital and integral part of the black family?" Pastors present the black church as more than just the religious and spiritual face of the black community. They say its outreach is pervasive in the black community and is reflected in the attitudes, values, and beliefs of African Americans. According to the pastors, the attitudes and feelings of African Americans flow largely from a series of social, economic, political, religious, and cultural relationships that have existed historically between African Americans and the black church. Not surprisingly,

Table 4.1
Role of the Church in the African-American Community

STATEMENT	Level of Agreement with Statement Percent Circling					
	Disagree 1	2	3	4	Agree Strongly 5	
1. The church has always been a central gathering place where black (or African) Americans could get together not only for worship but for other social and political activities.	4.7%	4.7%	12.9%	32.9%	45.6%	N=220 N=208
2. The church has been the primary liberator and educator of black (or African) Americans in the United States.	3.5%	4.6%	13.9%	36.4%	41.6%	N=210
3. Pastors are among the most informed persons in the black (or African-American) community and provide the most important source of leadership.	1.7%	9.8%	13.3%	35.3%	39.9%	N=210
4. The ties between the church and the family in the black (or African-American) community are so close that they are basically one and the same.	4.5%	16.4%	26.0%	26.0%	27.1%	N=214

the pastors see the church as central to the black experience and as providing social and cultural integration within the black community. Table 4.1 shows that church members share this perception of the centrality of the church and its importance to other institutions in the community. Only 4.7 percent of those surveyed circled 1 on the scale, while over 75 percent circled 4 or 5 in agreement with the statement that the church is central to the black community (statement 1, Table 4.1). Both the pastors and the congregations feel strongly that the church is a provider of educational, political, and social leadership (statements 2 and 3, Table 4.1). Although the strength of agreement is less than for the other statements in the table, the church is perceived by a majority the respondents as such a close extension of the black family that the two are seen as one entity (statement 4, Table 4.1). This same notion is articulated by the pastors when they are asked how the black church views its role in the black family.

These survey results support the views of the pastors as reported in the interviews. There is a consensus among the pastors that the church is very important in the black community and plays a major role in the black experience. On the whole, the surveyed congregations seem to be convinced of this importance. It should be noted, however, that the data do not indicate whether the same level of agreement would be found among blacks not belonging to the church or among white pastors and their congregations. This is an obvious limitation linked to the inability of encompassing such a complex issue into a single study.

In order to understand the social meaning of suicide in the black community, it is important to examine the extent to which the pastors' values, attitudes, beliefs, and norms that counter suicide are transmitted to and shared by others. This study suggests that they are transmitted and that congregants share considerable agreement with the pastors' views.

The pastors were asked: "What is your definition of suicide?"; "What is your attitude toward and theological view of suicide?"; and "What is your church's position on or attitude toward suicide?" Typical responses of the pastors underscore their personal and

Table 4.2
Religious Norms Concerning Suicide

STATEMENT	Level of Agreement with Statement Percent Circling					
	Disagree 1	2	3	4	Agree Strongly 5	
1. The taking of one's own life is not within the framework of God's perfect will.	9.6%	2.3%	9.0%	12.4%	66.7%	N=220 N=214
2. People who commit suicide lose their souls and spend eternity in hell.	4.0%	5.1%	20.5%	23.3%	47.2%	N=213
3. The use of alcohol and drugs is a type of suicide because it destroys the body, which is the temple of God.	10.6%	3.9%	5.6%	12.8%	67.0%	N=216
4. Black (or African) Americans have a tendency to cherish or place a higher value on life and on the family role than white Americans.	0.0%	15.8%	25.7%	35.7%	22.8%	N=208
5. There is some evidence that suicide may be increasing among black (or African) Americans. This is because of integration since the 1960s.	8.4%	18.5%	31.5%	22.5%	19.1%	N=215
6. Suicide has always been a "white thing" that black (or African) Americans just would not do.	3.4%	20.2%	25.3%	27.0%	24.2%	N=215

religious views of suicide. The pastors express an unequivocal condemnation of suicide as unacceptable, unimaginable, and sinful. The survey responses also clearly demonstrate a strong religious opposition to and condemnation of suicide among African Americans. Congregants believe that suicide is against God's will (statement 1, Table 4.2), and that those who commit suicide lose their souls and spend eternity in hell (statement 2, Table 4.2).

More than 75 percent of those surveyed indicate strong agreement (4 or 5 on the scale) with the statement that alcohol and drug use is a form of suicide (statement 3, Table 4.2). This view is consistent with the pastors' view of such behaviors as forms of suicide. However, when given an opportunity to be specific about what constitutes suicide, the pastors steer away from alcohol and drug use and define suicide as the deliberate taking of one's own life. They indicate no knowledge of anyone in their congregations who has attempted or committed suicide, yet they report knowledge of cases of drug abuse; the latter is felt to be a problem in the black community, but suicide is not.

Clearly, while pastors view alcohol and drug use as self-destructive behavior that could be viewed as a form of suicide, they distinguish such acts from the direct and intentional taking of one's life. The congregational respondents agree with the pastors that alcohol and drug use destroys the body and, therefore, is a type of suicide. The questionnaire did not give the respondents an opportunity to make the distinctions the pastors made, but presumably they would do so if given the chance.

The interview and survey results indicate that African Americans perceive themselves as uniquely different from their white counterparts: the pastors and their congregations believe that African Americans tend to place a higher value on life and on the role of the family than do white Americans (statement 4, Table 4.2). The pastors insist that suicide is a complete denial of the authority of God. Similarly, two-thirds of the congregants surveyed agree very strongly that suicide is not within the framework of God's perfect will (statement 1, Table 4.2).

The pastors tend to see increases in suicide as an outgrowth of racial integration. The survey respondents also feel that there has been some relationship between black suicides and integration since the 1960s, but they assign a lower score to their level of agreement with this item than with some other items (statement 5, Table 4.2).

When asked if they have knowledge of any suicides in their congregations, the pastors respond unanimously that they have no knowledge of any suicide or even attempted suicide in their congregations. However, nearly a third of the church members surveyed say they know of someone who has attempted suicide, and 16 percent state that they know of someone who has committed suicide (statements 19 and 20, Appendix G).

The congregants' answers may appear to conflict with the pastors'. But the pastors were asked if they had knowledge specifically of someone in their congregation who had either attempted or committed suicide, while the congregants were asked more generally whether they had knowledge of someone who had attempted or committed suicide. Therefore, that someone could be anyone: A nonblack, a noncongregant, or even the subject of a news report. Further, the congregants all could be referring to the same one or few cases of suicide or attempted suicide.

The interview responses show a consensus among the pastors that suicide is a "white thing," or a denial of what it means to be black; similarly, three-fourths of the congregants score 3 or higher in agreement with the statement that suicide always has been something that African Americans simply will not do. However, it should be noted that there is less strong agreement on this item than on those concerning theological views. While the pastors are unequivocal in their view of blacks and suicide, the congregants vary more in their responses (statement 6, Table 4.2).

The African-American experience has been wrought by violence: blacks, according to the pastors and about nine in ten of the congregants surveyed, are much more concerned about becoming victims of crime and drugs than of suicide (statement 6, Appendix G). Suicide has not been a part of their experience and therefore is not perceived by church leaders as a social problem having severe implications in the black community. When asked whether suicide has ever been discussed from the pulpit, the pastors are uniform in saying that suicide is not an issue in the black community and need not be a topic for church sermons. Violent crime and drugs, however, are so prevalent that they need to be frequent topics of church sermons and Bible-study discussions.

The contrasting beliefs regarding suicide versus drug abuse and violence were examined in the vignette section of the interviews. The survey questionnaire did not contain items reflecting the vignettes. Overall, however, the views expressed by the pastors are shared by the survey respondents. Their agreement is strongest on issues concerning religious beliefs about suicide and the significance of the church in the black community, and weakest regarding the uniqueness of suicide to whites. The disagreement on the latter issues, however, is relatively minor: the congregations largely agree that suicide simply is unacceptable among blacks.

Chapter 5

Conclusions, Limitations, and Implications

Although there have been increases in black suicide in the past two decades, the white suicide rate is still nearly double the black suicide rate for men and women. The question is, why is there relatively little black suicide? One persuasive answer that has been offered by scholars is that the black church and family provide amelioration or buffering of social forces that would otherwise promote suicide.

This book reports findings from a qualitative investigation of the hypothesis that suicide-buffering processes or factors can be found in the African-American community. Specifically, the focus is on the part played by the black church in constructing and reinforcing a particular social meaning of suicide that may act as a buffer against a higher prevalence of black suicide.

The low black suicide rate is well known and well documented. As shown in Chapter 1, there have been increases in black male suicides in the past two decades, but until the mid-1980s these were matched by increases in suicides among white males. Overall the white suicide rate is still nearly double the black suicide rate. The ratio of white male to black male suicide rates is 1.75 : 1, and the suicide rate among white women is more than double the rate for black women. While the low rate of suicide among black Americans may be one of the reasons that scholars have paid relatively little attention to the social forces leading to black suicide, it is this persistent difference in rates of suicide across racial groups that has been the focus of sociological interest in suicide in the black community.

Why is there relatively little black suicide? One answer is that those with lower status in society tend to direct aggression outward, while higher-status persons direct aggression inwardly (Henry and Short, 1965). The focus of this study, however, is on another persuasive answer found in the literature, that the low rate of black suicide is based in part on the role played by the black church and family in the African-American community in the amelioration or buffering of social forces that might otherwise promote suicide. To our knowledge, there has as yet been no direct investigation of the extent to which this persuasive answer is also a good one empirically.

Recall that the purpose of this book is to report a qualitative investigation of the notion that suicide-buffering processes or factors can be found in the African-American community. Specifically, the focus is on the part played by the church in constructing and reinforcing a particular social meaning of suicide (attitudes, norms, values, and beliefs) that may act as a counter or buffer against a higher prevalence of black suicide.

THE INFLUENCE OF THE CHURCH IN THE AFRICAN-AMERICAN COMMUNITY

The emphasis on church-based social meanings flows from the central role the church is believed to play in the black community. This centrality does not mean that the influence is one-way, but the literature describes the influence of the church as pervasive in the black community. The church has maintained its traditional status within the African-American community. Moreover, its influence has not been confined only to the African-American community. It has also been seen as providing moral, social, and political leadership in the larger community.

Values, norms, attitudes, and beliefs concerning suicide among African Americans in general, and not just those actively involved in church, have their origin in the church. Staples (1976) and

Wilmore (1983) argue that religious participation is a major way in which the morals, ethics, self-definition, and cultural traditions of blacks are expressed. The literature supports the notion that religious precepts and practices are deeply woven into the social fabric of the African-American community.

The moral and social views promulgated by church leaders and adhered to by active church participants should influence the values of the larger black community. Although my own observations of and participation in the black community, and the responses of informants in this study, lend credence to that influence in the community studied, I do not attempt specifically to demonstrate it. Rather I begin with the description in the literature of the significance of the black church in the life of the community, and ask: is the social meaning of suicide reflected in religious views in such a way that, if the church does have the significance attributed to it in the black community, it would be expected to work against black suicide? If so, how might the normative view of suicide differ from that of other forms of deviance and life-threatening behavior, such as violence, crime, and drug abuse, which are not lower in the black community?

Black suicides may be expressions of fatalism, as Durkheim's (1951) brief reference to suicide and slavery would suggest. If so, do the low rates of suicide reflect low rates of fatalism, in spite of continuing objective conditions that would seem to work against hope? Do integration and regulation through forced division of labor, in Durkheim's terms, keep egoistic and anomic suicide low in the African-American community?

One application of the Durkheimian perspective that has become part of the literature on black suicide follows the reasoning in Merton's (1938) anomie theory and depicts relative deprivation and blocked opportunity as producing strain, stress, and alienation in the black community. This high level of anomie is expected to result in high rates of all forms of deviance. The rates of violence, crime, and drug abuse in the black population are seen as relatively high and, therefore, meet the expectations. That suicide is not high seems to run counter to the theoretical expectation; this discrepancy is accounted for by reference to the church and other institutions as providing internal integration and a buffer against the anomic forces that might foster suicide. It is this perspective that forms the specific framework for this book.

The hypothesis in the literature, then, is that social forces buffering against black suicide are especially to be found in the values and norms of the church and family in the African-American community. Although there have been recent changes undermining it, the African-American family historically has shown amazing resiliency under very stressful and debilitating conditions (Wilson, 1988). Strong family ties and traditions have persevered. The church as an institution also has traditionally played a unifying and leadership role in the African-American community. The hypothesized buffering effect of the church in the black community makes sociological sense. As we have seen, it has been stated in one form or another in previous literature, but there has been no empirical research specifically focused on it. The state of knowledge in this area of research, therefore, is still very much underdeveloped. The research presented here should be treated as exploratory rather than as a precise testing of the hypothesis.

In the interviews, the pastors offer strong support for the contention that the church serves unifying and leadership functions in the black community. They point to the black church as an institution that has provided social and cultural integration for black Americans, and has interacted with the black family to provide resiliency under stressful conditions.

This perceived significance of the church in the community does not guarantee that the church's views on suicide are widespread in black culture. However, the literature strongly supports this perception, and it seems reasonable to assume that the norms and attitudes expressed by the pastors are reflected to some extent in the larger community.

The pastors' views appear to be consistent with the hypothesis that religious norms in the black community play a buffering role against higher prevalence of suicide. Those norms, as iterated by the pastors in this study, condemn suicide on religious grounds and define it as so alien to the black experience, both religious and secular, that willingness to commit suicide runs directly counter to all that is implicit in what it means to be African American.

PERCEPTIONS OF SUBSTANCE ABUSE AND SUICIDE

Emile Durkheim defined suicide as "all cases of death resulting directly or indirectly from a positive or negative act of the victim himself, which he knows will produce this result" (Durkheim, 1951, p. 44). The definition of suicide expressed in the interviews with pastors is consistent with this basic conception of suicide. The pastors consider suicide to be "willful, premeditated and not in accord with a sound judgment," or a "nonproductive act whereby a person takes his or her own life." In addition, the responses of some of the pastors to the general questions and to the vignettes refer to self-injurious behavior, such as drug use, as a less clearly deliberate form of suicide.

Yet, this fusing together of suicide and other self-injurious acts seems only to be a way of showing that one can be self-destructive without really intending to be. The pastors quickly make distinctions between this "slow suicide" and "actual" suicide, which they maintain throughout the interviews. They do see a difference between intended suicide as the deliberate and immediate taking of one's own life, and other actions such as drug taking. The pastors obviously do not consider them to be the same thing because they report no knowledge of suicides or suicide attempts in their congregations, but are aware of cases of drug and alcohol abuse. Moreover, the pastors' responses to the vignettes distinguish between suicide as deliberately ending one's life and alcohol or drug abuse. The latter is viewed as very wrong but an understandable response to the socioeconomic and political condition of blacks in American society; suicide is defined as unthinkable for black people.

The pastors were not asked direct questions about their views on and explanations for other forms of deviance in the black community as they were about suicide, but those views were clearly stated in response to the third and fourth vignettes (see appendix D). The pastors clearly deplore the use of alcohol and drugs, but there is a subtle shift from the way in which they condemn suicide. This shift does not seem to be in the degree to which suicide and drug abuse are condemned. Rather, it appears to be the extent to which there are references to conditions or uncontrollable factors that may move one to crime and drugs. The behavior is seen as unacceptable, but understandable because of the system and social conditions, unemployment, lack of education, influence of friends, and so on.

This perception of substance abuse as unacceptable but understandable lends some insight into how the church's normative influence may aid in keeping the suicide rate low while seeming to have less of an impact on other forms of deviance. This same perceptual shading is evident in the assessment given of the vignette depicting a homicide by a youngster with a history of crime (see appendix D). The pastors are unanimous in condemning the behavior and viewing it as extremely serious, but as with the case of drug abuse, they tend to offer plausible explanations for it.

The pastors' basic view of crime, murder, and drug abuse is similar to their basic view of suicide; all are sins. However, they tend to assess violence and substance abuse as stemming from environmental factors, societal conditions, economic deprivation, and failure to provide black families with the services and benefits that are afforded to white families. But these same adverse conditions can be overcome without resorting to suicide. The pastors neither excuse nor justify violent behavior against others or the self-destructive behavior of alcohol and drug abuse. But they see them as explicable in the face of deprivation, while suicide is inexplicable in the face of the same deprivation.

PERCEPTIONS OF SUICIDE IN THE AFRICAN-AMERICAN COMMUNITY

This is not to say that the informants have no conception of the social causes of suicide; when asked specifically to elaborate on this point, their replies are very sociological. All of the pastors point out that suicide is a very infrequent pulpit topic. Most do not ever preach on it. They see this lack of direct pastoral attention to the issue as a natural outcome of the low level of suicide in the black community. There are many pressing spiritual and social problems that need frequent addressing from the pulpit, but suicide is not one of them.

The pastors were asked why they believe that suicide is less of a problem for the African-American community, and why suicide occurs on those infrequent times when it is committed. Their explanations for black suicide are consistent with the deprivation and deficit theories noted above, namely that the person committing suicide has experienced a breakdown in religious and family ties, and a buildup of stress, associated with the assimilative effect of racial integration, which is seen as undermining the internal integration of the black community. But this still leaves us with the question of why the suicide rate among blacks remains low.

One major set of answers, which we have just reviewed above, has to do with the influence of the specifically religious norms concerning the unexcusable and inexplicable nature of suicide. But another answer implied in the pastors' responses seems to reflect a fusion of these religious norms with secular influences. The message in these views is that suicide, in addition to being unholy and sinful, is almost a complete denial of black identity and culture. It is assumed that suicide is outside the black experience. It is simply not done. In the revealing words of the first pastor interviewed, which inspired the focus of this book, "suicide is a white thing."

Suicide is viewed as a white phenomenon not simply because of its recognized greater statistical frequency among whites. Rather the phrase captures the idea that suicide is antithetical to black culture. This was communicated to the researcher, who is black, not only by the first pastor, but several others in subsequent interviews. They insisted that he should not even have to ask questions related to blacks and suicide because suicide is a white thing, not a black thing.

An aversion to suicide is so much an assumed part of being black that the pastors were a bit surprised to have the topic raised, especially by another black person. It is not just an assumed part of being a black religious person. It is assumed about all blacks. The pastors knew that the interviewer is religiously committed and an active participant in his own church, and the topic at hand was religious beliefs on suicide. Nevertheless, the pastors did not say, "You should know suicide is unthinkable, you're a Christian." Rather they said, "You should know that, you're black." The truth is that the interviewer, himself, took it so much for granted, and was so focused on the content of the religious norms themselves, that the cultural assumption that suicide is a "white thing" was not explicitly recognized before beginning the research. The idea that this assumption may interact with religious norms as part of the cultural buffers against suicide in the black community was a serendipitous outcome of the interviews.

Pastors are unanimously of the opinion that some of the same difficulties and problems that might lead to suicide by whites do not pose such a threat for African Americans. The belief is that, if anything, economic, political, and social deprivation has made black Americans more resilient, but that racial integration may break down some of that resiliency because white attitudes about suicide may be taken on.

Of course, suicide is condemned by whites as well, and the religious beliefs of white Christians regarding suicide probably do not differ much from the beliefs of black Christians expressed by the pastors in this study. However, the significance of the church in the black community is hypothesized to result in a more pervasive and stronger influence of those beliefs than in the white community.

The concept that whites are fundamentally different in terms of their response to stress is clearly articulated by the pastors in this study. Through the "struggle" black Americans have developed a culture of resilience to behavior that would otherwise be self-destructive. The perception of blacks as being a more religious people than their white counterparts is pervasive in the African-American community. African Americans are described, by pastors and their congregations, as being able to endure more hardships and not succumb to the despair and despondency that lead other racial and ethnic groups to suicide. Being black in America is a lifelong struggle. Additionally, being able to endure life in the black community is a struggle. The church is the centerpiece within the black experience that has unified black Americans around a common tradition shaped out of suffering. It is the institution that has provided strength, identity, coping skills, and hope. To those who lead and belong to the black church, this common bond and source of strength have meant that suicide is not a part of what it means to be black. Whites may do it, but blacks do not.

CONCLUSIONS

There have been some recent changes in suicide rates, and the difference for black and white males ages twenty-five to thirty-four is not great. But there is no question that the overall rate of suicide among white Americans is still about double the rate for black Americans. The question addressed here is why there is so little black suicide. The principal goal of this study was to investigate the extent to which some empirical support for the working hypothesis can be found. Emphasis was placed on the role of the black church, in particular, in transmitting and reinforcing a particular normative climate and social meaning of suicide that may sustain a lower rate of suicide than might otherwise be expected.

Thirty pastors in one community in a southeastern state were interviewed to elicit their observations and views on suicide in the black community as compared to other forms of deviance, such as crime and drug abuse. According to the pastors, the church is a refuge in the community, problem solver, integrator, and moral voice of the black community. They describe the church as central to the black experience, which is consistent with what sociologists of race and ethnicity have been saying for a long time. Assuming the importance of the black church in the larger community as asserted by these pastors, and as stated in the literature, the question becomes; can religiously based attitudes, values, norms, and beliefs be identified that would appear to have an impact on suicidal behavior in the black community? I believe that the findings in this research offer a tentative affirmative reply to the question.

There is reason to believe, based on the interview findings, that there are religious norms against suicide, with secular modifications and applications. The nature of these beliefs offers some insights into why they may be expected to buffer against suicide, but not against other forms of deviance. The pastors condemn suicide as an unpardonable sin. Theologically, they define it as an unpardonable sin "against God's perfect will." Suicide does nothing for the soul except place it in peril of eternal damnation. The church recognizes no justification for suicide.

Crime and drug abuse are also strongly condemned as immoral, but the pastors offer explanations for these actions that differ somewhat from the unequivocal condemnation of suicide. They tend to place some blame on the system, and hence deflect some of the responsibility away from the individual. They do not condone or overtly excuse criminal and drug behavior, but given the circumstances that many blacks face (e.g., economic, political, and social deprivation) they seem to understand how a black person could succumb. Those same circumstances, while recognized as sometimes being factors in suicide, are never referred to as making suicide understandable.

The secular side of the beliefs about suicide is that suicide is inherently contradictory to the black experience, and is a complete denial of black identity and culture. The pastors reason: "Why talk about suicide?" Not concentrating on suicide in sermons, they feel, is not an oversight; suicide just is not a problem. The factors that lead to suicide among whites do not pose a threat to black Americans. Blacks have developed an apparent resilience to that self-destructive behavior. To struggle and endure hardship toughens one to withstand sorrows, and religious faith offers hope and the promise of a better life. Suicide is seen as peculiar to white America "across the tracks." Black Americans may get involved in crime and drug abuse, but "to our credit at least we don't kill ourselves." That's a "white thing."

The limitations of this study are obvious. It is a small-scale, qualitative investigation in one southern community. It provides no direct comparison with white informants and does not include a sample of the general black population. There are factors in black suicide beyond the buffering effect of moral norms and values, and the study does not touch on them. Therefore, there is no claim to have provided a definitive answer to the question of how important the black church has been in keeping the prevalence of suicide among blacks low. However, the study does offer some evidence on the hypothesis, and moves us closer to good answers. It offers a basis for tentative conclusions about the empirical reality of a religiously influenced normative climate or set of social meanings that defines suicide as counter to God's will and as unacceptable, perhaps even unthinkable, for black Americans. The hypothesis that this has helped to restrain suicide in the black community by buffering against other factors that may induce motivation to suicide thus becomes more plausible. That hypothesis now needs to be tested in larger cities with more systematic data and representative samples, and with suitable comparisons with the white community.

The low black suicide rate is well documented. There have been increases in black male suicides in the past two decades, but until the mid-1980s that was matched by increases in suicides among white males. The differences in suicide between younger black and white males has never been large. Nevertheless, overall the white suicide rate is nearly double the black suicide rate. The ratio of white male to black male suicide rates is 1.75:1, and the suicide rate among white women is more than double the rate for black women (Department of Health and Human Services, 1992). It is this persistent difference in rates of suicide across racial groups that has been the focus of sociological interest in suicide in the black community. The question raised by this difference is: Why is there relatively little black suicide?

The question is raised because there seem to be reasons to expect higher levels of suicides among blacks. Durkheim's (1951) brief reference to suicide and slavery would suggest that "fatalistic" suicide should be high in the black community. Recall that socio-logical theories and studies of suicide have been influenced heavily by Durkheim, and that this study began with a Durkheimian perspective. Durkheim reasoned that suicide was a social phenom-enon. He proposed four categories of suicide: egoistic, anomic, altruistic, and fatalistic. These categories are contingent upon the degree and nature of individual integration into and regulation by the social collective. Egoistic suicide results from a weakening and loss of close social ties to groups and collectivities. At the other extreme, altruistic suicide results from excessive identification with and integration into a collectivity. Anomic suicide is the result of the individual's normlessness and lack of regulation. Fatalistic suicide is the polar opposite of anomic suicide; it is the result of excessive regulation.

Durkheim's theory appears to have undergone at least two interpretations relevant to the question of black suicide. The first departs from Durkheim's original four causes of suicide; the second follows Durkheimian tradition more closely. Those adher-ing to the first interpretation follow a "one-cause" argument, combining both regulation and integration into a focus on social integration or disorganization (Cavan, 1928; Merton, 1938; Cloward and Ohlin, 1961). Cavan (1928) explains suicide in terms of the amount of anomie or personal disorganization experienced by the individual. This notion would lead one to expect high rates of deviance, including suicide, among blacks, since powerlessness, hopelessness, and social disorganization characterize many seg-ments of the African-American community.

Merton (1938) proposes that high rates of deviance among lower-class and minority groups occur when these groups fail to achieve cultural goals of success. According to anomie theory, relative deprivation and blocked opportunity (conditions found in the lower-class and black community) produce strain, stress, and alienation leading to all forms of deviance (Merton, 1938). Similarly, Cohen (1955) and later Cloward and Ohlin (1961) attribute higher rates of deviance in the lower-class structure to status frustration and blocked opportunity in trying to meet legitimate demands of middle-class standards. All of the usual indices of anomie or social disorganization (e.g., dysfunctional families, powerlessness, high illegitimacy rate, alienation, unemployment, blocked opportunity) are found disproportionately among the black community. Feelings of powerlessness and oppression have long been offered as reasons why blacks commit suicide (Prudhomme, 1938; Davis, 1980a, pp. 228–229; Little, 1983, p. 142; Gibbs, 1988, p. 272; Moss, 1991, p. 292). If this is so, to the extent that perceptions of powerlessness permeate the black community, the suicide rate should be higher than it is.

Other theorists follow more closely Durkheim's original theory of integration and regulation, and stress excessive regulation (Henry and Short, 1965; Maris, 1969; Breed, 1970). Henry and Short (1965) reason that high rates of deviance can be explained in terms of "external restraints." Outward aggression and violence toward others, rather than self-destructive behavior, result when external restraint is high. Hence, greater external restraint in the lower-class substructure results in a lower suicide rate. Maris (1969) refers to "external constraints," or lack of social integration, to explain suicide. High external constraints reduce the likelihood of suicide. Breed (1970) views black suicide as fatalistic, based on the Durkheimian idea of excessive regulation and forced division of labor.

Higher black suicide rates are also suggested by "family deficit" theory. The frequent absence of a male role model in the black family is seen as one such deficit. The role of black females as head of households is hypothesized to maximize the propensity toward suicide (Davis, 1979, 1980a, 1980b, 1982). For black youths the absence or loss of a "sensitive, strong, loving masculine father figure causes psychological damage and leads to suicide" (Hendin, 1969, pp. 407–422). Davis proposes that suicide among African Americans is likely to occur with the weakening of the relational, communal, and family system and that "the likelihood of suicide is increased without important support systems" (Davis, 1980b, p. 228).

That the influence of the black church on suicide may be important in the black community would seem to follow from both of these perspectives. According to the anomie and social disorganization argument, something in the black community must counter the anomic effects on blacks; this role is hypothesized to be played by the church. If the external constraint and fatalism argument is emphasized, one may look to the church as providing mechanical solidarity and hope.

A review of the literature concerning the effect of the church on the low suicide rate among African Americans indicates that researchers adhere more closely to the anomie and social disorganization perspective. According to the literature, suicide rates are low because the church and other institutions (e.g., family and social organizations) provide social interaction, which in turn acts as a buffer against the greater prevalence of suicide in the black community that otherwise would be expected.

By focusing on that body of literature, this study uncovered religious meanings that counter suicidal tendencies. The study was primarily qualitative and ethnographic, aiming to understand whether the black church plays the suicide-ameliorating role hypothesized for it. Pastors served as knowledgeable informants who could provide information on the social meaning of suicide in the black community. Data were collected primarily through face-to-face interviews with thirty black pastors, who first were asked general questions on suicide and then were asked to respond to vignettes depicting situations involving suicide, drug use, and crime. In addition, survey questionnaires were administered to the members of six church congregations, yielding a total sample of 220 persons. The goal of the interviews and survey was to examine the extent to which church-based views and norms in the black community buffer against a greater prevalence of suicide.

The focus of the interviews was on religious and normative views of suicide, the relationship between the black church and family, and the extent to which church-based attitudes and norms opposing suicide are transmitted in church. The interviews were designed to solicit the pastors' opinions on suicide and other forms of deviance, such as crime and drug abuse, in the black community. There was a high level of agreement among the pastors. The literature on black suicide suggests that the church is pervasive in the black community and that its influence is an important factor in low suicide rates among African Americans. The pastors offer the same view.

According to the pastors, the church is a refuge, a problem-solver, an integrator, and the moral voice of the black community. Hence, the church helps to unify the social bonds within the black community. The pastors see the church as central to the black experience. This unity is promoted through the interplay of church and family. The prevailing attitude of the pastors is that "the church is our mother," "the church and family are one," and that the church "acts to keep the family together." All of the pastors believe that the church meets the emotional and spiritual needs of its members. Unquestionably, the pastors believe that the church has molded the black family. Given the importance of the church to the black experience as proposed in the literature and by these pastors, a question arises: do church-based attitudes, values, norms, and beliefs have an impact on suicidal behavior in the black community?

The pastors' answers are affirmative. The interview results clearly suggest that the church's influence creates buffers against suicide among African Americans. The nature of the pastors' views on suicide provides insight into why the church helps to mitigate suicide but not other forms of deviance. The pastors condemn suicide as an unpardonable sin, as a "white thing" alien to the black experience. The congregations share their pastors' views, albeit with somewhat less conviction.

Suicide is defined as unpardonable, unforgivable, and even unthinkable for blacks. Theologically, the pastors view suicide as being sinful and against God's will. This notion of suicide as sinful appears to be pervasive in the black community. Suicide puts the soul in peril of eternal damnation; it is perceived as that which impedes the individual from fulfilling what God intended. The church recognizes no justification for suicide.

Although they know of no suicide cases among their congregations, the pastors offer two possible explanations for suicide among African Americans. The first is a breakdown in religious values and family ties. The second explanation cites the effects of racial integration. The belief is that blacks have assimilated white materialistic values, thus weakening ties in the black community and making African Americans more susceptible to committing suicide. Violence in general is perceived by the pastors as a by-product of assimilation through racial integration, and the fact that the black suicide rate remains relatively low is a reflection of the religious and secular norms of the black community.

Ultimately, suicide is perceived by the pastors and by a majority of the congregants as alien to the black experience. Pastors do not discuss the issue of suicide from their pulpits. Suicide is viewed as a complete denial of black identity. Pastors unanimously share the belief that some of the problems that lead to suicide by whites simply do not pose a threat to blacks. This belief is shared by most members of their respective congregations.

Blacks have developed an apparent resilience to self-destructive behavior. Their struggle and endurance of hardship have toughened them and allowed them to withstand sorrow—their religious faith gives them hope and the promise of a better life. The church stands as a bastion in the struggle: it strengthens and bonds blacks in a tradition shaped from suffering. The church leaders point to the church as being primarily responsible for providing the cultural integration, hope, and resiliency that, in turn, act as buffers against black suicide.

Responses to the vignettes were analyzed to determine the difference between the normative climate for suicide and that for other forms of destructive behavior, including drug abuse and violence, which are relatively common in the black community. While the pastors strongly and unequivocally condemn crime and drug use as well as suicide, they offer subtle rationalization for crime and drug use. Given the circumstances of the black community (e.g., economic, political, and social deprivation), they can "understand" such criminal behavior, but those same circumstances are never applied to the justification of suicide.

A review of the surveys reveals that church members share the beliefs of their pastors, although their level of agreement varies. Church members believe that religion is central to the black experience and is responsible for unifying the black community. A vast majority believe that the strength of the church lies in its close relationship with the family—so close, in fact, that the two are seen as one entity. Respondents overwhelmingly condemn suicide and believe that it is against God's will. Suicide remains an unpardonable sin for which one is sentenced to damnation. The congregations also believe that blacks place a higher premium on life than do whites (statement 8, appendix G). To pastors and congregations alike, suicide is a "white thing."

To the extent, then, that this shared social meaning of suicide radiates out into the black community, it appears to play a role in keeping the black suicide rate low, thus allowing the conclusion that empirical support exists for the working hypothesis with which this study began.

Limitations and Implications for Future Research

This conclusion is qualified by the limitations of the research. The most obvious shortcoming of this study lies in the self-selected, or volunteer, nature of the sample, with regard both to the interview informants and to the survey respondents. Not everyone wanted to talk with the researcher. Hence, the sampling procedure of this study essentially was based upon the self-limiting nature of the number of people contacted. The high illiteracy rate among African Americans also affected the way in which data could be gathered. The instructions for completion of the questionnaire were not clear to some respondents; therefore, interpretation of the survey results is limited by some uncertainty about the meaning of the responses on the five-point scale.

The limitations of the study are obvious. It is a small-scale, qualitative investigation in one southern community. It provides no direct comparison with white informants and does not include a sample of the general black population. There are factors in black suicide beyond the buffering of moral norms and values, and the study does not touch on them. Therefore, there is no claim to have provided a test of the buffering hypothesis. However, the study has provided evidence of a religiously influenced social meaning of suicide as unacceptable, perhaps even unthinkable, for black Americans. This permits us to go beyond the general hypothesis of the suicide-buffering function of the religious institution in the black community found in the literature to propose the specific hypothesis that the condemnation of suicide as wrong and an unthinkable contradiction of black culture is sufficiently pervasive in the black community that it helps to keep the rate of suicide low.

There is nothing in the hypothesis which assumes that adherence to the suicide beliefs expressed by the pastors in this study is uniform in the black community. Variations in commitment to them may be related to the age and sex differences in suicide among blacks, since it is likely that religious influence is stronger on women and older African Americans. The next steps are to conduct research on the buffering hypothesis in larger cities with quantitative data, representative samples, and suitable comparisons with the white community.

Little (1983) argues that the overall low suicide rate among blacks is due to the high death rate among young black males: by the time the black population matures, those who would commit suicide either have been murdered or have killed themselves through drug abuse. Seiden (1982) proposes a "survivor hypothesis," in which only the strongest African Americans survive. Another scholar agrees: "By the time those blacks reach senior citizen years, they have developed such a repertoire of coping strategies and have so many support mechanisms in an extended family network that suicide is not considered" (Blackwell, 1985, pp. 334–35). Moreover, it is suggested that whites do not confront the same social structure that generates deviance among African Americans.

Future research might test these demographic hypotheses by comparing black and white death rates due to all unnatural causes (e.g., homicide, drug abuse, and traffic fatalities). The demographic argument suggests that the total death rate for young blacks is greater than that for young whites. If such were the case, then those blacks (i.e., those who are prone to violence or otherwise are risk-takers) who would commit suicide in later years would not survive, and elderly black suicide rates would remain low. To the extent that young whites have a better survival rate, more of them are still around to be vulnerable to suicide in their later years, thus the positive relationship between age and suicide for whites. Yet another line of research could investigate Seiden's "survivor hypothesis," which states that the coping strategies and repertoire of young blacks are less developed and significantly different from those of older blacks.

Durkheim (1951) proposed that poverty was in itself regulative under certain conditions. Another plausible hypothesis, therefore, is that a forced division of labor and poverty are regulative, and that whites in similar situations also would have low rates of suicide. Future research could test this hypothesis in a highly regulated environment, such as a prison, which is essentially the same for both blacks and whites. If the social meaning of suicide defined in the present study by black pastors and church members holds more generally among blacks, then findings in a prison study would reflect those in the black community. In other words, black inmate suicide rates would be lower than white inmate suicide rates, and suicide would be considered a "white thing" by black inmates even in a social system where both blacks and whites are highly regulated.

The data from the interviews and surveys in this study provide support for a tentative conclusion about the socially integrative, suicide-buffering forces operating in at least a significant portion of the African-American community: the black church provides a normative climate that helps to keep the black suicide rate relatively low. This theory-guided research goes beyond what is currently available in the literature, and should provide the basis for further testing of its tentative conclusions.

Appendix A: Letter of Introduction

Dear Pastor:

This is to affirm that Kevin Early is a doctoral candidate in sociology in the process of carrying out his dissertation project. I am his advisor and chairman of his dissertation committee. His research project has been approved by this committee and the Department of Sociology. In our judgment the project is a significant one capable of contributing to knowledge and understanding of an important social issue. His research will investigate suicide and other life threatening behavior and the role that the church has played or could play in dealing with these social issues.

As a Pastor you are in a key position to offer insights and observations to aid his research. I would very much appreciate your kind cooperation in granting him a private and confidential interview to learn of your views on these matters.

Mr. Early will contact you personally. If you have any questions of me regarding him or the project, please do not hesitate to call me at 392–0265.

Sincerely,

Ronald L. Akers
Professor of Sociology

Appendix B: Explanation of Study Letter

Dear Pastor:

I am a candidate for the Ph.D. degree in Sociology at the University of Florida writing a dissertation on the causes and prevention of suicide (as well as other life threatening behavior such as drugs) in the African-American community. The enclosed correspondence from Dr. Ronald L. Akers, Professor of Sociology at the University of Florida, confirms my status as a doctoral student, as well as the nature of my research.

I feel that this study will provide invaluable information, as it is a study of the African-American church, examining its values, norms, beliefs, and social relations as related to these social issues.

This study will involve interviews with African-American pastors in Gainesville. I am writing to ask for your participation by granting me an interview. The interview will be approximately one hour. Confidentiality will be maintained.

Your participation in this study is critical. A follow-up phone call will be made to you to answer any questions you have about the study and to schedule appointments.

Thank you for your cooperation.

With kindest regards, I am

Sincerely,

Kevin E. Early

Appendix C: Interview Schedule

1. What is your definition of suicide?
2. What is your attitude and theological view of suicide?
3. What is your church's position or attitude toward suicide?
4. Do you have knowledge of any member of your church congregation attempting or committing suicide?
5. What were the circumstances?
6. What is the role of religion within your community?
7. What is the role of the black church in the black community?
8. Is the black church a vital and integral part of the black family?
9. Do you have contact with your members on a regular basis?
10. How much does the church involve the family into its activities?
11. How does the black church view its role in the black family?
12. Has suicide ever been discussed from the pulpit?
13. What would you do if a member of your congregation talked about suicide?
14. What are the family activities or family centered activities in the church?
15. How do you encourage youth involvement and participation?
16. How are you involved in local community politics?
17. How are you involved in the "War on Drugs"?

Appendix D: Vignettes

SITUATION 1

A church mother, whom you have known for years, has changed since her husband of forty years committed suicide after learning that he had prostate cancer. She stays relatively to herself, has dropped out of church activities, has lost weight, and appears unkempt. At first you thought that her behavior was typical of mourning, but it has now been well over a year since her husband's demise and she appears to be getting worse instead of better.

1. What would you say about her husband's suicide?
2. How do you define this person's suicide?
3. How would the church respond to the widow?
4. Where would you start in handling this situation?
5. In what context as a clergyman would you talk to this person?
6. What step or action would you likely take to help get this woman re-directed or re-integrated into the church family?
7. Suppose you could have encountered her husband before his suicide?

SITUATION 2

A fifteen year old youth has reacted badly to his parent's divorce some months ago. Always extroverted, the child is now quiet and withdrawn. In school the child isolates himself from his peers and has dropped off the basketball team. His friends avoid him and his grades have dropped. His father was always active in his life, and you suspect that he feels abandoned by him. His mother, with whom he lives, tends to let him alone, to do whatever he wants. The child has told a school counselor that he is tired of living and that he would like to go to a far away problem-free place where he can find ultimate peace. The child insists that he is the reason that his parents aren't living together. He believes that the divorce would not have occurred if his parents really loved him. Frustrated, the child has come to you to tell you of his attempts to find a way to "escape from it all." Crying and rolling up his sleeves slowly, the child reveals scars where he has slashed his wrists several times.

1. What is your analysis of the problem?
2. Talk to me like you would talk to that boy regarding suicide.
3. How would you approach this boy's mentioning of suicide as a pastor?
4. How would you evaluate the seriousness of the situation?

SITUATION 3

Ernest is a twenty-eight year old, single, unemployed man who has a problem with alcohol and multiple drug abuse (marijuana, Quaaludes, and crack). Ernest grew up in the church. He was baptized, sang in the youth choir, and always attended Sunday school and church services with his family. His family is still an active part of your congregation. Ernest, on the other hand, spends most of his time drinking very heavily with only several short periods of being sober. Ernest is still living at home with his parents. According to his mother, he comes and goes as he pleases. Ernest has been arrested several times by the local police and his drivers license was suspended over a year ago for driving while intoxicated. When Ernest is sober he makes an occasional appearance in church. However, when he is "high" he gets together with his old friends who, like him, misuse alcohol and drugs. Ernest needs help and his parents have asked you to intervene.

1. How would you evaluate the seriousness of the situation and what would you do about it?

2. How would you evaluate Ernest's behavior?

3. What steps or action would you take as pastor to re-direct or re-integrate Ernest into the church family?

4. Talk to me like you would talk to Ernest.

SITUATION 4

Charles is an eighteen-year-old youth who has just been arrested and charged with the murder of another youth. Charles grew up in the black community in Gainesville where he lived with his mother, a member of your church, and five siblings. Charles never knew his father, as his father abandoned his mother when he was an infant. As the oldest of six children, Charles spent most of his time caring for his younger brothers and sisters while his mother worked as a janitor in a downtown bank. Charles was an average student in high school until he dropped out in his junior year. He claims that he dropped out of school for good reasons. Frustrated, Charles began acting out at home and stealing from his mother's purse. Finally, Charles' mother told him to either get a job or go back to school where he could get his diploma. Unable to get a job, Charles got involved in law violations.

1. How would you evaluate Charles' behavior?

2. How would you evaluate the seriousness of Charles' situation?

3. In your role as a clergyman, how would you approach this situation?

4. What steps would you take or action would you likely take to re-direct the youth into the church family?

Appendix E: Survey

Some of the questions are statement opinions. For these, please express, on a five-point scale from 1 to 5, the extent of your agreement with each of the statements on your own personal feelings. [In response to questions the following instructions were given: If you circle 1 that means you disagree with the statement. Please circle one of the other four numbers if you agree with the statement.]

DIRECTIONS: Please do not write your name on this survey. Therefore, feel free to be very honest. Indicate your responses by circling the appropriate answer. You may skip any question that you do not wish to answer.

What is your denomination?

Adventist AME Baptist CME Methodist Pentecostal

What is your present age?

Under 18 19–28 29–37 38–45 46 or older

What is your sex?

Male Female

What is your present marital status?

Single Married Divorced

1. The taking of one's own life is not within the framework of God's perfect will.

   1 2 3 4 5

2. The use of alcohol and drugs is a type of suicide because it destroys the body, which is the temple of God.

   1   2   3   4   5

3. There is some evidence that suicide may be increasing among black (or African) Americans. This is because of integration since the 1960s.

   1   2   3   4   5

4. The church has always been a central gathering place where black (or African) Americans could get together not only for worship but for other social and political activities.

   1   2   3   4   5

5. People who commit suicide lose their souls and spend eternity in hell.

   1   2   3   4   5

6. Black (or African) Americans are much more concerned about becoming victims of crime and drugs than becoming victims of suicide.

   1   2   3   4   5

7. Black (or African) Americans are more likely to commit crimes against other black Americans than against white Americans because the penalties are not as severe.

   1   2   3   4   5

8. Black (or African) Americans have a tendency to cherish or place a higher value on life and on the family role than white Americans.

   1   2   3   4   5

9. The ties between the church and the family in the black (or African) American community are so close that they are basically one and the same.

   1   2   3   4   5

10. Suicide has always been a "white thing" that black (or African) Americans just would not do.

    1   2   3   4   5

11. The church has been the primary liberator and educator of black (or African) Americans in the United States.

    1 2 3 4 5

12. Pastors are among the most informed persons in the black (or African-American) community and provide the most important source of leadership.

    1 2 3 4 5

13. At this church, suicide is seldom mentioned in sermons from the pulpit or in Bible study.

    1 2 3 4 5

14. At this church, the problem of violent crime and drugs in the black (or African-American) community is frequently a topic of sermons or discussion in Bible study.

    1 2 3 4 5

15. There are many family-oriented activities in this church.

    1 2 3 4 5

16. Youth involvement and participation is encouraged in the church.

    1 2 3 4 5

17. The pastor is actively involved in community politics.

    1 2 3 4 5

18. The pastor is actively involved in the "War on Drugs."

    1 2 3 4 5

19. Do you have knowledge of someone who has attempted suicide?

    none   1 person   2 persons   3 or more persons

20. Do you have knowledge of someone who has committed suicide?

    none   1 person   2 persons   3 or more persons

Appendix F: Informed Consent

(Read to all respondents at the beginning of the session.)

My name is Kevin E. Early. I am a doctoral candidate in sociology at the University of Florida. I am conducting a study to investigate suicide and other life threatening behavior within the black (or African) American community. My focus is on the role that the African-American church has played or could play in dealing with these social issues.

A questionnaire will be distributed to each member of the congregation. I will give you instructions for filling it out in a moment. Please mark your answers directly on the survey sheets. After completing the survey, please turn the surveys in to me or to the ushers before I leave the sanctuary.

Remember, you are a volunteer in this project and you may withdraw at any time. You may skip any question that you do not wish to answer. Please do not write your name on the surveys. This procedure assures anonymity of responses so that you may feel free to answer as you honestly feel. Your responses are anonymous. By completing the surveys you are giving your consent to participate.

NO MONETARY AWARDS FOR YOUR PARTICIPATION ARE INVOLVED.

Thank you very much for your participation.

Kevin E. Early
Principal Investigator
Department of Sociology

Appendix G: Survey Results

Denomination	Percent
Adventist	19.2
African Methodist Episcopal (AME)	20.9
Baptist	13.7
Christian Methodist Episcopal (CME)	1.1
United Methodist	17.6
Pentecostal	27.5
Age	
Under 18	14.9
19–28	15.5
29–37	28.8
38–45	12.6
46 or older	28.2
Sex	
Male	27.2
Female	72.8
Marital Status	
Single	34.9
Married	55.8
Divorced	9.3

| | Disagree |
| STATEMENT | 1 |

1. The taking of one's own life
   is not within the framework
   of God's perfect will.   9.6%

2. The use of alcohol and drugs
   is a type of suicide because
   it destroys the body, which
   is the temple of God.   10.6%

3. There is some evidence that
   suicide may be increasing
   among black (or African)
   Americans. This is because
   of integration since the
   1960s.   8.4%

4. The church has always been
   a central gathering place
   where black (or African)
   Americans could get together
   not only for worship, but
   for other social and
   political activities.   4.7%

5. People who commit suicide
   lose their souls and spend
   eternity in hell.   4.0%

6. Black (or African) Americans
   are much more concerned about
   becoming victims of crime and
   drugs than becoming victims
   of suicide.   5.1%

	2	3	4	Agree Strongly 5	N=220
	2.3%	9.0%	12.4%	66.7%	N=214
	3.9%	5.6%	12.8%	67.0%	N=216
	18.5%	31.5%	22.5%	19.1%	N=215
	4.7%	12.9%	32.2%	45.6%	N=208
	5.1%	20.5%	23.3%	47.2%	N=213
	5.6%	19.7%	33.1%	36.5%	N=215

| | Disagree |
| STATEMENT | 1 |

7. Black (or African) Americans
    are more likely to commit
    crimes against other black
    Americans than against white
    Americans because the
    penalties are not as severe.   5.6%

8. Black (or African) Americans
    have a tendency to cherish
    or place a higher value on
    life and on the family role
    than white Americans.   0.0%

9. The ties between the church
    and the family in the black
    (or African-American)
    community are so close that
    they are basically one and
    the same.   4.5%

10. Suicide has always been a
    "white thing" that black
    (or African) Americans just
    would not do.   3.4%

11. The church has been the
    primary liberator and
    educator of black (or African)
    Americans in the United
    States.   3.5%

	2	3	4	Agree Strongly 5	N=220
	10.7%	23.6%	29.2%	30.9%	N=215
	15.8%	25.7%	35.7%	22.8%	N=208
	16.4%	26.0%	26.0%	27.1%	N=214
	20.2%	25.3%	27.0%	23.6%	N=215
	4.6%	13.9%	36.4%	41.6%	N=210

| | Disagree
1 |
STATEMENT	
12. Pastors are among the most informed persons in the black (or African-American) community and provide the most important source of leadership.	1.7%
13. At this church, suicide is seldom mentioned in sermons from the pulpit or in Bible study.	13.3%
14. At this church, the problem of violent crime and drugs in the black (or African-American) community is frequently a topic of sermons or discussion in Bible study.	7.0%
15. There are many family-oriented activities in this church.	3.6%
16. Youth involvement and participation is encouraged in the church.	2.3%
17. The pastor is actively involved in community politics.	.6%

	2	3	4	Agree Strongly 5	N=220
	9.8%	13.3%	35.3%	39.9%	N=210
	10.4%	19.1%	27.7%	29.5%	N=210
	12.8%	20.3%	28.5%	31.4%	N=209
	6.0%	16.8%	36.5%	37.1%	N=204
	4.1%	7.6%	27.3%	58.7%	N=209
	10.8%	14.4%	23.4%	50.9%	N=204

		Disagree 1
STATEMENT		
18.	The pastor is actively involved in the "War on Drugs."	1.8%

19.	Do you have knowledge of someone who has attempted suicide?	67.4%
20.	Do you have knowledge of someone who has committed suicide?	84.2%

			Agree Strongly	
2	3	4	5	N=220
5.9%	20.6%	28.2%	43.5%	N=207

1 person	2 persons	< 3 persons	
19.1%	6.7%	6.2%	N=215
9.0%	3.4%	3.4%	N=214

Appendix H: Methodology

The study was conducted in a southeastern Standard Metropolitan Statistical Area (SMSA) of about 84,770 with 21 percent African Americans. The data were collected by face-to-face interviews with black pastors and a questionnaire survey of church members. A total of thirty-seven black churches were located in the area and thirty pastors agreed to take part in the study. The churches of the pastors interviewed ranged in memberships from 45 to 340. The pastors were interviewed as informants, as persons strategically located in the community to provide information, insight, and contacts within that community. The interviews were loosely structured and undisguised, lasting about one and one-half hours each.

The first general part of the interviews covered four general areas:

1. The pastor's views as leader of the church and the stated position of his or her church on suicide.
2. The pastor's assessment of the role of the church and religion in the African-American family and community.
3. The extent to which the pastor teaches and preaches on suicide-relevant topics.
4. Information about the pastor's view of the causes and prevention of suicide and assessment of why there are few suicide deaths in the African-American community.

The second part of the interview followed up on these general questions with presentation of two vignettes depicting cases of suicide and attempted suicide and two vignettes depicting cases of crime and substance abuse (see appendix D). Each vignette was succeeded by four to seven follow-up questions which were designed to elicit pastors' judgments and attitudes about several issues related to the nature of suicide and life-threatening behavior such as drug abuse and violence, and the role that the black church could play or has played in dealing with these social issues.

None of the pastors reported direct experience with cases of suicide in their congregations, and therefore responses to actual cases could not be used. The vignettes allowed me to explore what the reactions and assessment would have been if the pastors had encountered such cases. The vignettes regarding other types of deviant behavior were presented to provide something against which to judge the views on suicide. The vignettes allowed the researcher to contrast the views on suicide expressed by the church leaders with views on crime and violence (threatening life of others), and drug abuse (which could be life-threatening to oneself). The idea was to discern whether there was something about the content of those views that seemed to run counter to pressures toward suicide more than they countered pressures toward violence or drugs.

SAMPLES AND DATA COLLECTION PROCEDURES

The researcher is an accepted member and active participant in the black community of Gainesville, Florida. Participation in and integration into the religious life of the community provided the researcher access to shared symbols, language, and common understandings. The specific methods utilized to collect data for this study consisted of:

1. Face-to-face interviews with pastors, which included

    (a) general questions about views of suicide and

    (b) vignettes to allow comparison of views of suicide with views of other deviant behaviors such as crime and drug abuse;

2. A questionnaire survey administered to church members.

The interview and questionnaire were designed to elicit attitudes, opinions, and beliefs of African Americans toward suicide and how they have responded or would respond to attempted suicide and to the families in which suicide has occurred. The goal of the interview and question-naire procedures was to examine the extent to which social processes and norms in the black community foster lower-than-average suicide rates.

INTERVIEWS WITH PASTORS

In order to determine the number of black churches in the city of Gainesville, the researcher contacted the mayor's office. That office directed the researcher to Gainesville's affirmative action office for a computerized list of all black churches and pastors in metropolitan Gainesville. The list included thirty-seven churches. Pastors of each of the thirty-seven churches were notified by letter and later by a follow-up telephone call. Except for conflicting schedules, no unusual problems arose in arranging the interviews. Of the thirty-seven pastors asked to participate, thirty responded favorably and seven declined. Of the thirty pastor-informants, twenty-nine were male and one was female.

The researcher's acceptance in the religious life of the African-American community was of great value, but did not guarantee success in gaining cooperation. In order to secure the confidence of the interview subjects, considerable thought was given to the interview approach. The success of the approach was evidenced by the number of people that cooperated with the study. Several criteria were utilized in the approach. First, the interviews were not attempted unless the subject had time to complete the interview without any unusual interruptions. Second, the interviews were private and confidential so as to encourage truthful answers. Third, the subjects were told why the information was wanted and how it would be used.

A letter of introduction (see appendix A), together with a brief expla-nation of the study (see appendix B) was mailed to church pastors. A follow-up phone call was made to confirm receipt of the letter and to schedule an interview.

The pastors were interviewed as informants, not as respondents. That is, they were relied upon not just for their individual attitudes and characteristics, but for their ability to provide information, insight, and contacts within their communities.

Interviews were conducted from June to November 1990. The initial intention was to conduct three interviews per week, but because twenty-six of the thirty subjects were "weekend" pastors who held other full-time jobs, interviews had to be scheduled around the pastors' individual work hours, thus limiting the weekly time available for interviews. The bulk of the interviews were conducted on Wednesday, Thursday, and Friday mornings (in some cases the researcher reported to nonchurch job sites to conduct the interviews). Other interviews were conducted on Sundays after church services. For the most part, pastors were cooperative in making and keeping their appointments.

Interviews (see appendix C) were approximately one to one and one half hours in length. Some, however, exceeded three hours because of the depth of the pastors' responses or because of occasional interruptions (e.g., phone calls, visits by congregants). Interviews were conducted in the pastors' offices of the medium- and large-sized churches. Small-church interviews were conducted in the church sanctuaries. Only four interviews were conducted in pastors' homes, and two at the pastors' nonchurch job sites.

The nature of the interviews required that they be conducted skillfully and sensitively. It was important that the informant feel comfortable in the situation and trust the researcher. The interviewing technique was loosely structured and undisguised, thus allowing the pastors latitude to develop their thinking.

The interviews began with a discussion of general issues followed by the four vignettes related to suicide and other deviant behaviors (see appendix D). The researcher read each vignette to the pastors and then asked four to seven follow-up questions designed to elicit the pastors' opinions and attitudes concerning the behaviors displayed in the vignettes.

SURVEY OF CHURCH MEMBERS

A short questionnaire (see appendix E) was distributed directly to church members. Six churches were selected for the survey: two small churches (fewer than one-hundred members), two moderately sized churches (one-hundred to two-hundred members), and two larger churches (more than two-hundred members). Most of the surveys were conducted in conjunction with church services, but not before the researcher had actively participated in the services. At one church, for example, the researcher was asked to help raise the offering and bless the collection. At another, he was asked to give testimony, or to witness.

Overall, the researcher participated in and attended at least twenty youth-day and family-day services, building-fund campaigns, and worship services. This involvement in the religious life of the community fostered rapport and established credibility with the congregants and provided the researcher with additional insights into their community.

Prior to distribution of the questionnaire, church pastors were asked to announce that a study of suicide and other life-threatening behaviors among African Americans was being conducted in the Gainesville area. The pastors then introduced the researcher, who in turn talked about the survey, provided instructions on filling out the questionnaire, and read a consent notice (see appendix F) while church ushers distributed pencils and the questionnaires. Survey time was approximately one hour. Questionnaires and pencils were collected by ushers following the worship services.

Congregants were asked about their religious beliefs and about the attitude of their respective churches toward suicide. They also were asked about their handling or knowledge of suicides or attempted suicides within their family, church, and community.

Once pastor interviews and congregant surveys were completed, they could be examined for consistency under the working hypothesis. Could the expressed values, norms, beliefs, and social relations possibly act to ameliorate anomie and buffer against suicide in ways so specific that they do not buffer against other forms of deviance?

The data from the surveys were used more descriptively than inferentially. That is, the data were not submitted to bivariate or multivariate statistical analysis of sociodemographic or other variables to account for differing opinions and attitudes among the people in the study. Rather, the focus was on using the data to describe the degree of consistency among African-Americans' views on and reactions to suicide.

RELIABILITY, VALIDITY, AND LIMITATIONS

Ethnographic reliability focuses on the data-gathering technique and consistency. That is, it insures that if the study were conducted by someone else in a similar manner, similar findings would be obtained. Ethnographic validity refers to the degree to which participant observation and interview techniques achieve what they purport to discover—an accurate representation of what is occurring within the social situation or system being studied (LeCompte and Goetz, 1982, pp. 31–60; Plummer, 1983, p. 101). In a qualitative study involving interviews, validity is proportional to the researcher's understanding of the meanings of the observed sociocultural experience. Hence, response validity for this study is based on the researcher's prolonged involvement in the observed culture, and on the credibility of the researcher to the informants.

This study was limited by the self-selected or volunteer nature of the population with regard to both the interview informants and the survey respondents. The high illiteracy rate among African Americans in the community affected the way in which the researcher gathered the data, and not everyone approached agreed to take part in the study. Consequently, the motive to use interviews rather than questionnaires as the major information-gathering instrument becomes evident. Precautions were taken to ensure that the oral and written instructions were clear and that no actions or questions on the researcher's part would influence the opinions of the interview or survey subject. Every effort was made to encourage sincere responses.

These limitations do not preclude a set of data that should provide a sufficiently clear basis for tentative conclusions about the socially integrative, suicide-buffering processes operating in at least a significant portion of the African-American community. This is theory-guided research that goes beyond what is currently available in the literature, and it should provide the basis for further testing of its tentative conclusions.

References

Akers, R. 1985. *Deviant behavior.* 3d ed. Belmont, CA: Wadsworth.

Allen, N. 1977. History and background of suicidology. In *Suicide: Assessment and intervention,* ed. C. L. Hatton, S. M. Valente, and A. Rink, 1–15. New York: Appleton-Century-Crofts.

Allen, W. 1978. Black family research in the United States: A review, assessment and extension. *Journal of Comparative Family Studies* 9:168–89.

Aron, R. 1967. *Main currents in sociological thought.* New York: Basic Books.

Billingsley, A. 1968. *Black families in white America.* Englewood Cliffs, NJ: Prentice-Hall.

Blackwell, J. 1985. *The black community: Diversity and unity.* New York: Harper & Row.

Bogadus, E. 1966. *The development of social thought.* New York: David McKay.

Bohannan, P. 1960. *African homicide and suicide.* Princeton, NJ: Princeton University Press.

Breed, W. 1966. Suicide, migration, and race: A study of cases in New Orleans. *Journal of Social Issues* 22:30–43.

Breed, W. 1970. The Negro and fatalistic suicide. *Pacific Sociological Review* 13(1–4):156–62.

Brenner, M. 1985. Intensive interviewing. In *The research interview: Uses and approaches,* ed. M. Brenner, J. Brown, and D. Carter, 147–61. 3d ed. London: Academic Press.

Bush, J. 1976. Suicide and blacks: A conceptual framework. *Suicide and Life-threatening Behavior* 6(4):216–22.

Cavan, R. 1928. *Suicide.* Chicago: University of Chicago Press.

Choron, J. 1972. *Suicide.* New York: Charles Scribner's Sons.

Christian, E. 1977. Black suicide. In *Suicide: Assessment and intervention,* ed. C. L. Hatton, S. M. Valente, and A. Rink, 143–159. New York: Appleton-Century-Crofts.

Clark, K. 1965. *Dark ghetto.* New York: Harper & Row.

Cloward, R., and Ohlin, L. 1961. *Delinquency and opportunity.* Glencoe, IL: The Free Press.

Cohen, A. 1955. *Delinquent boys.* Glencoe, IL: The Free Press.

Comer, J. 1973. Black suicide: A hidden crisis. *Urban Health* 2:3–15.

Davis, R. 1978. Dimensions of black suicide: A theoretical model. *Suicide and Life-threatening Behavior* 8(3):161–73.

Davis, R. 1979. Black suicide in the seventies: Current trends. *Suicide and Life-threatening Behavior* 9(3):131–40.

Davis, R. 1980a. Black suicide and the relational system: Theoretical and empirical implications of communal and familial ties. *Research in Race and Ethnic Relations* 2:43–71.

Davis, R. 1980b. Suicide among young blacks: Trends and perspective. *Phylon* 41(3):223–29.

Davis, R. 1982. Black suicide and social support systems: An overview and some implications for mental health practitioners. *Phylon* 43(4):307–14.

Department of Health and Human Services. 1991. *Statistical series, Annual data, 1990.* Series E-21. Washington, DC: Government Printing Office.

Douglas, J. 1967. *The social meaning of suicide.* Princeton, NJ: Princeton University Press.

Douglas, J. 1968. The sociological analysis of the social meaning of suicide. In *International encyclopedia of the social sciences,* ed. David L. Sills, 375–84. New York: The Free Press.

Dreger, R., and Miller, K. 1968. Comparative psychological studies of Negroes and whites in the United States: 1959–1965. *Psychological Bulletin Monograph Supplement* 70(3):1–58.

Durkheim, E. 1933. *The Division of labor in society.* Trans. G. Simpson. New York: The Free Press. (Originally published in 1893.)

Durkheim, E. 1951. *Suicide.* Ed. George Simpson. Glencoe, IL: The Free Press. (Originally published in 1897.)

Feagin, J. 1989. *Race and ethnic relations.* 3d ed. Englewood Cliffs, NJ: Prentice-Hall.

Gibbs, J. 1968. Introduction. In *Suicide,* ed. J. P. Gibbs, 1–19. New York: Harper & Row.

Gibbs, J. 1984. Black adolescents and youth: An endangered species. *American Journal of Orthopsychiatry* 54(1):6–21.

Gibbs, J. 1988. *Young, black, and male in America.* Dover, MA: Auburn House.

Gibbs, J., and Martin, W. 1971. Status integration and suicide. In *The sociology of suicide,* ed. Anthony Giddens, 14–30. London: Frank Case.

Giddens, A. 1965. The suicide problem in French sociology. *British Journal of Sociology* 16(1):3–15.

Giddens, A. 1971. *The sociology of suicide.* London: Frank Case.

Glasgow, D. 1981. *The black underclass.* New York: Vintage Books.

Gold, H. 1982. *The sociology of urban life.* Englewood Cliffs, NJ: Prentice-Hall.

Halbwachs, M. 1971. The causes of suicide. In *The sociology of suicide,* ed. Anthony Giddens, 10–23. London: Frank Case. (Originally published in 1930.)

Hendin, H. 1969. Black suicide. *Archives of General Psychiatry* 21:407–22.

Hendin, H. 1978. Suicide: The psychosocial dimensions. *Suicide and Life-threatening Behavior* 8(2):99–117.

Henry, A., and Short, J. 1965. *Suicide and homicide: Some economic, sociological, and psychological aspects of aggression.* New York: The Free Press.

Hill, R. 1972. *The strengths of black families.* New York: Emerson Hall.

Holinger, P., and Offer, D. 1982. Prediction of adolescent suicide: A population model. *American Journal of Psychiatry* 139(3):302–7.

Johnson, B. 1965. Durkheim's one cause of suicide. *American Sociological Review* 30(6):875–886.

Johnson, C., and McKenney, N. 1974. Population composition: National origin, race, and religion. In U.S. Bureau of the Census, *Current population reports,* series P-23, no. 49, *Population of the United States, trends, and prospects: 1950–1990,* 88–99. Washington, DC: Government Printing Office.

Kiev, A., and Anumonye, A. 1976. Suicidal behavior in a black ghetto. *International Journal of Mental Health* 5(2):50–59.

LeCompte, M., and Goetz, J. 1982. Problems of reliability and validity in ethnographic research. *Review of Educational Research* 52(1):31–60.

Lincoln, C. E. 1974. *The black church since Frazier.* New York: Schocken Books.

Liska, A. 1981. *Perspectives on deviance.* Englewood Cliffs, NJ: Prentice-Hall.

Little, C. 1983. *Understanding deviance and control.* Itasca, IL: F. E. Peacock.

Lukes, S. 1972. *Emile Durkheim: His life and his work.* New York: Harper & Row.

McAdoo, H. 1981. *Black families.* 2d ed. Beverly Hills, CA: Sage Publications.

McLean, H. 1963. The emotional health of Negroes. In *Mental Health and Segregation,* ed. M. Grossack, 131–39. New York: Springer.

Maris, R. 1969. *Social forces in urban suicide.* Homewood, IL: The Dorsey Press.

Maris, R. 1985. The adolescent suicide problem. *Suicide and Life-threatening Behavior* 15(2):91–109.

Martin, E., and Martin, J. 1978. *The black extended family.* Chicago: University of Chicago Press.

Merton, R. 1938. Social structure and anomie. *American Sociological Review* 3(4):672–82.

Moss, J. 1991. Hurling oppression: Overcoming anomie and self-hatred. In *Black male adolescents: Parenting and education in community context,* ed. Benjamin P. Bowser, 282–97. New York: University Press of America.

National Center for Health Statistics. 1992. *Vital Statistics of the United States,* Vol. II, *Mortality, Part A, 1950–1989.* Hyattsville, MD: Public Health Service.

National Center for Health Statistics. 1990. *Health, United States, 1989.* DHHS Pub. No. (PHS) 90–1232. Hyattsville, MD: Public Health Service.

Nisbet, R. 1966. *The sociological tradition.* New York: Basic Books.

Parsons, T. 1968. Emile Durkheim. In *International encyclopedia of the social sciences,* ed. David L. Sills, 311–19. New York: The Free Press.

Plummer, K. 1983. *Documents of life.* London: George Allen & Unwin.

Pope, W. 1976. *Durkheim's suicide*. Chicago: University of Chicago Press.

Poussaint, A. 1977. Rising suicide rates among blacks. *Urban League Review* 3(1):22–30.

Powell, E. 1958. Occupation, status and suicide: Toward a re-definition of anomie. *American Sociological Review* 23(2):131–39.

Prudhomme, C. 1938. The problem of suicide in the American Negro. *Psychoanalytic Review* 25:187–204, 372–91.

Ritzer, George. 1988. *Sociological theory*. 2d ed. New York: Alfred A. Knopf.

Roberts, A. 1975. Self-destruction by one's own hand: Suicide and suicide prevention. In *Self-destructive behavior*, ed. A. R. Roberts, 21–77. Springfield, IL: Charles C. Thomas.

Rutter, M. 1985. Resilience in the face of adversity. *British Journal of Psychiatry* 147:598–611.

Salter, D. 1978. Personality differences between suicidal blacks: An exploratory study. *Dissertation Abstracts International* 38:7–13.

Schultz, D. 1969. *Coming up black: Patterns of ghetto socialization*. Englewood Cliffs, NJ: Prentice-Hall.

Seiden, R. 1970. We're driving young blacks to suicide. *Psychology Today* 4(3):24–28.

Seiden, R. 1972. Why are suicides of young blacks increasing? *Health Services and Mental Health Administration* 87:3–8.

Seiden, R. 1982. Mellowing with age: Factors influencing the non-white suicide rate. *International Journal of Aging and Human Development* 13(4):265–84.

Stack, C. 1974. *All our kin*. New York: Harper & Row.

Staples, R. 1975a. Suicide and black youth. *The Black Scholar* 6(1):30–39.

Staples, R. 1975b. To be young, black and oppressed. *The Black Scholar* 7(4):2–9.

Staples, R. 1976. *Introduction to black sociology*. New York: McGraw-Hill.

Steele, R. 1972. Suicide in the black community. *Renaissance* 2(2):15–24.

Swanson, W., and Breed, W. 1976. Black suicide in New Orleans. In *Suicidology: Contemporary developments*, ed. E. S. Shneidman, 99–128. New York: Grum & Stratton.

Timasheff, N. 1967. *Sociological theory: Its nature and growth.* New York: Random House.

Turner, J., and Beeghley, L. 1981. *The emergence of sociological theory.* Homewood, IL: The Dorsey Press.

U.S. Bureau of the Census. 1986. *Reports of the secretary's task force on black and minority health.* Vol. 5. Washington, DC: Government Printing Office.

Wekstein, L. 1979. *Handbook of suicidology.* New York: Brunner/Mazel.

Wilmore, G. 1983. *Black religion and black radicalism.* 2d ed. Maryknoll, NY: Orbis Books.

Wilson, W. 1988. The ghetto underclass and the social transformation of the inner city. *The Black Scholar* 19(3):10–17.

Wilson, W., and Aponte, R. 1985. Urban poverty. *Annual Review of Sociology* 11:231–58.

Woodford, J. 1965. Why Negro suicides are increasing. *Ebony* 20(9):89–100.

Index

About the Author

KEVIN E. EARLY is an Assistant Professor of Sociology at Oakland University, Rochester, Michigan. He specializes in criminology and the study of deviance and social control.